THE CLARION CALL

Redeeming African Nations beyond Rhetoric and Religion

CHRIS LEO

Copyright © 2022

By Chris Leo

palacemedia338@gmail.com

All Rights Reserved

TABLE OF CONTENTS

INTRODUCTION 4

CHAPTER ONE 8
AWAKE! O SLEEPER! 8
   SLEEPING GIANTS.. 13
   WHY GIANTS ARE ASLEEP 31
   WHY SLEEPING GIANTS MUST AWAKE....................... 42
   WHAT HAPPENS WHEN THEY ARE AWAKE? 56

CHAPTER TWO 66
ARISE, O COMPATRIOT! 66
   ARISE FROM THE DEAD 67
   SEEKING THE LIVING AMONG THE DEAD 77
   REASONS AND RESULTS OF SEEKING THE LIVING AMONG THE DEAD 89

CHAPTER THREE 98
THE CLARION CALL 98
   THE NECESSITY OF THE CALL 99

CHAPTER FOUR 116
HEED THE CALL... 116

CHAPTER FIVE 124
RANDOM PERSPECTIVES 124

REFERENCES... 131

INTRODUCTION

When we carefully consider the many things that go on around us in our families, communities, constituencies and country, we are often thrown into a state of helplessness and hopelessness. The emergencies that erupt, the challenges that crop up and the pressure to respond that is on all of us who are concerned minds – all these testing our faith and loyalty to God and to our fatherland.

The insufficient infrastructures to enhance our quick resolve to lend help, and the motivation to try being muffled by forces beyond us, we seem to sink deeper into this artificially created abyss of hopelessness. When this is allowed to go on for too long a time, the situation will appears irredeemable and irreversible.

With the spate of hideous atrocities being committed on the soils of the Nigerian state and the African space coupled with the lame response by those in authority at different levels especially at the top echelon, the need to step in and tame the tide cannot be over-emphasized at a time like this.

The falling standard in education, the rising debt profile of the nation, the increasing torment of poverty in the Cush continent, the continued degrading and watering down of our moral and religious codes, the alarming rate of impunity by public and political office holders across board, and the worsening state of insecurity have drawn a red line of battle with our collective existence such that men and women of good conscience cannot keep mute any longer. Men and women who have been endowed with rare godly abilities and incorruptible tenets are being expected to rise to the occasion.

When I survey the scenarios and evaluate the enormous human and natural resources at our disposal, only one conclusion comes to my mind: the giants are sleeping! And this is the time to awake them out of their sleep and slumber. So, I embark on writing this book.

This book highlights the features of the Nigerian National Anthem and Pledge, as the giant of Africa. These two national creeds provide the pivot for balancing my arguments with my thoughts, some schools of thoughts and the realities around us. We shall look into the call for compatriots to arise, why sleeping is no longer a pleasurable option and what happens when these men awake and arise from their slumber. The necessity for this all-important call and the crucial need to heed it have been highlighted here as well.

As a minister unto God and men, the Word of God as contained in the Holy Bible forms my strong reference base. So, as my tradition is, I give credence to the records of Biblical history to authenticate this clarion call. It is important to note that nothing happens behind the Almighty God. He has always offered humanity the privilege of being part of the mission to redeem or salvage their world.

What many have done at best is to receive this offer but are yet to respond faithfully to it. This is a time to reconsider that summon to service, which this books seeks to provide and prepare ourselves to respond in ways that will ensure the mission is accomplished. This is because the mission to save what is left is only possible when we heed the call and join the redeemers' camp.

Chris Leo Nwachukwu
November 2016

CHAPTER ONE
AWAKE! O SLEEPER!

The Nigerian National Anthem has two verses or stanzas. The first verse begins with "Arise O Compatriots" – a call to duty, while the second one opens with "O God of Creation" – a prayer to the Almighty God, the Designer of the country. That means the National Anthem is a combination of a call to duty and a prayer for help. One is directed to Nigerians while the other to God to help Nigerians who would respond to the call to fulfil the focus of the call. If you ask me, it is quite interesting and in order – a call to duty and a prayer for help to perform the duty.

I believe that this Anthem was written by the inspiration of God. Whoever coined those words and drafted those beautiful lines of inspiring charge must have drawn inspiration from the Holy Bible. I strongly believe this to be so because I am a Christian who have read and still reads the Bible. So, I am surely convinced that those lines came from the Spirit of God.

A careful look at the Anthem and its exegesis would buttress my assertion. For want of doubt, let us look at the lines here.

Arise O Compatriots! Nigeria's call obey

To serve our fatherland, with love and strength and faith

The labours of our heroes past, shall never be in vain

To serve with heart and might, one nation bound in freedom

Peace and unity.

O God of Creation, direct our noble cause

Guide our leaders right, help our youths the truth to know

In love and honesty to grow, and living just and true

Great lofty heights attain, to be a nation where peace

And justice shall reign.

These lines could only have been possible with the help of the Holy Spirit of God and they truly convey the mind of God for any country. With a call to duty and a solemn prayer to God as we have them, no nation is expected to go wrong or live below excellence. But quite the opposite has been our experience in this beautiful country.

The reason is that both the leaders and the followers no longer see it a big deal to reflect periodically on those thought-provoking lines in order to evoke the sweet memories that once resonated our minds.

These are memories of living in a peaceful, fruitful and prosperous land with boundless opportunities for growth and development. The memories which the selfless struggles of our founding fathers stirred in our hearts as they harped on the milk and honey that would flow for generations to come when they sought the collective support of the people in achieving independence from the British colonial masters.

These beautiful memories have long been eroded by the many frightening and ferocious activities that greet the people of this country every morning and evening. They have been replaced with heart-rending, mind-dulling and spirit-sapping memories that are worse than the nightmares one gets after seeing a Hollywood horror movie at midnight. A very pathetic sight, to say the least!

The first line of our National Anthem reads: Arise O Compatriots, Nigeria's call obey! The first word here is, **"Arise".** This implies that someone might be lying down, sleeping or not sitting up. The word is a command, more than an appeal. It is more of an instruction than an advice. "Arise" is not in any way a suggestion, so does not give anyone the pleasure or privilege to choose to obey or not. To arise is a divine command to all Nigerians at home and abroad to respond to without further hesitation.

However, before one can arise and respond to the command, one needs to comprehend the issues at stake. This means that the people to whom the command is given should be conscious of what is in the offing. And to be conscious requires that one is aware of the things happening in the country and then prepare to get involved. It so seems to me that some people, who are not aware or conscious and so have not comprehended the urgency of the hour, are in slumber or asleep. Hence, a man who is asleep needs to awake in order to comprehend the need to arise and answer the call.

One of the greatest apostles of God, Paul of Tarsus, saw the rot in Ephesus, a city reputed for its grandeur worship of the goddess Artemis (Diana) which the people believed to bring them fortune and increase in their merchandise. Paul saw how the Christian believers lived almost in passivity and others in cold complicity. Then, he wrote them his letter and cried out, *"…Awake, O sleeper, and arise from the dead, and Christ shall shine (make day dawn) upon you and give you light. Look carefully then how you walk! Live purposefully and worthily and accurately, not as the unwise and witless, but as wise (sensible, intelligent people), making the very most of the time [buying up each opportunity], because the days are evil"* (Ephesians 5:14-16 AMP).

That was the admonition the great apostle Paul gave to the brethren at Ephesus, and by extension, to us. And by the grace and mandate of God upon me, I am giving the same admonition to all Nigerians.

There are two words of command used in the above piece of Bible history – awake and arise. Paul cried out, **"Awake O sleeper…!"** This is the cry of the moment to Nigerians: Awake O Nigerians! Our National Anthem urges or commands us to arise, but before one can arise, he needs to first of all awake.

To awake is to come to grips with oneself; to come to terms with the brazen realities of the moment. It means to become conscious of what is at stake – the urgency of the hour. To awake means to become aware of the dire situations on ground; to acknowledge the realities and to do something about them. To awake implies also that someone has been sleeping on duty. To awake could also mean that though one is not sleeping, he is in a slumber and needs to be aroused to action.

There has been commotion in the country: insecurity, joblessness, hunger, poor education, injustice and delayed justice, massive looting of the nation's treasuries, etc., and some people who have been heavily endowed to provide solution have gone to sleep. Among the few who seem to be awake, some have been thrown into a state of docility, negligence and apathy.

The feeling of hopelessness has engulfed the society such that many bright minds that are being looked unto have been thrown into despair. The degree of wantonness perpetuated by custodians of the nation's treasury has reached the high heavens, thus requires that someone must awake to save what is left. So, in essence, to awake connotes that there is fire on the mountain and someone needs to put it out.

SLEEPING GIANTS

"Awake O Sleeper and arise…" suggests many things. From a general perspective and comprehension, it gives the idea that someone is sleeping when there is need to be awake and at work. But in my view, it goes beyond that. One, it reveals that the situation of the time in which he is sleeping is a dicey one that requires all men to be awake and alive to responsibility. Two, it reveals that the sleeper could be someone who is being looked unto to remedy the situation. Three, it reveals that the sleeper has been sleeping for a long time such that he is being thought and seen as dead.

That probably is the reason for the additional call to arise from the dead.

So, going with this analogy, the sleeper is someone we can describe as a giant. And because he is sleeping, we can as well call him the sleeping giant. A sleeping giant is someone who has got the muscles to fix the manpower deficits in building solid structures or infrastructure in his community, but has relaxed them.

A sleeping giant is one with brainpower to fix the leadership, economic, and social demerits of his nation, but has chosen rather to keep it redundant. He is one who has got the spiritual endowment to bring deliverance to his land, but has chosen to confine such privileged gift of Heaven within his immediate family or within the walls of his religious environment.

When God blesses a man with unusual strength like Samson, it is to make manpower requirements easier for his community. This is why the Philistines presented Goliath against the armies of Israel. One man against an army of men! They knew what one man with awesome manpower or muscles could do. The presence of Goliath sent quivers down the spines of all the soldiers of Israel such that not even their chief general, King Saul could muster the courage to face and fight him. So, for forty days, the Philistine giant paraded himself in front of the armies of a whole nation without anyone with the liver to respond to the challenge.

Now, imagine if Goliath was sleeping at the time of the challenge; the time he was really needed, victory would have been in favour of the Israelites in a matter of days. This is because the Israeli army would have capitalized on the fact that God was with them to fight their enemies and finished them off in one blow. But even though they had God in their camp, solidly behind them, they could not still summon the needed courage to face their enemies. Why? Because the presence of one man with huge muscles sent the giants of God's own country into sleeping! The same goes for any other nation, Nigeria in particular.

When God blesses a man with unusual, extraordinary brainpower, expectations are that he uses it to help in solving some problems in his domain that require the use of brains! Economic issues, diplomatic bias, and environmental challenges that confront the people and query their intelligence are easily addressed by these men with brainpower. But whereby these men lock up this God-given asset and ingenuity and choose to watch from the sides while their nation goes to ruin economically and diplomatically, they become sleeping giants.

When God endows a man with the ability and courage to speak out against injustice, impunity and other ignoble acts carried out against humanity, and all he cares for is his own safety, then such a man has failed and is a perfect example of a sleeping giant.

When God endows and empowers a man or a woman with grace, nay, with uncommon grace to intercede for divine intervention in the land, and such people keep mute or perhaps only look after their congregation, they are no better than sleeping giants. And they are worse than sleeping giants if in the midst of chaos and crisis as we have been seeing in this country, they maintain the dumb status quo. Whether he is a pastor of a church or a president of a country, a legislator or a litigator, a servant or a master, truth is that such a man is a disappointment to his Creator and to his nation. Arise, O Sleeper!

God never leaves any nation without men and women who can remedy ugly situations. In every nation under heaven, there are people who have been endowed with wisdom, intelligence and ability to direct others in the paths to follow. They have the courage to confront daring situations, scale any mountains, and subdue them. God our Creator generously invested in man far higher dominion over his environment.

Man is king over his environment and god to the earth as God is King over all Universe and God of all gods. Therefore, he is expected to rule as king and reign as god – to bring all other elements of creation under control and to ensure the smooth-running of the entire earthly system.

Man is required by the tenets of creation to take charge and fix any area of human existence that goes out of joint. This expectation is not rocket science. Even though it is not a simple task to be in charge of one's environment with so many uncertainties evidenced with daily interruptions and disruptions in human relations, yet it is a mission that is possible. This is because it is divinely ordained by God.

The truth is that those disruptions are man-made. So, it means that man is the architect of his challenges and problems and therefore can solve these problems if he so desires. The challenges that nature bequeaths man are such that God has empowered man to solve. This means that the expectation of God from man is just and in order – not one that should keep him down, but stir up the giant and greatness in him.

If human beings can still manufacture and fly rockets to the outer space, then no excuse should be given for failing to rise to fix any disjointed areas of life. After all, the breakfast of champions according to one author is solving problems. But when champions become threatened by problems and shrink back, they end up as sleeping giants.

Sleeping giants are not only those whose natural or supernatural endowments are very obvious and conspicuous. There are people who lack muscles to rise to physical challenges facing their communities or country but they can develop their own kind of muscle by stirring up what is in them. The case of David and Goliath teaches us that intelligence outranks muscles any day as affirmed by the writer of the Book of Proverbs, Solomon of Israel. As soon as David saw the uncircumcised giant of the Philistines, the giant in him awoke and roared.

"As they talked, behold, Goliath, the champion, the Philistine of Gath, came forth from the Philistine ranks and spoke the same words as before, and David heard him. And all the men (or army) of Israel, when they saw the man, fled from him, terrified. And the Israelites said, Have you seen this man who has come out? Surely he has come out to defy Israel... And David said to the men standing by him, What shall be done for the man who kills this Philistine and takes away the reproach from Israel? For who is this uncircumcised Philistine that he should defy the armies of the living God? David said to Saul, Let no man's heart fail because of this

Philistine; your servant will go out and fight with him" (2 Samuel 17:23-26, 32 AMP).

While the giants on the battle ground went into hiding, the one that has been in the bush, responded to the challenge of the hour. General Saul's men were all soldiers but the giant in them went asleep in a time their country needed warriors to defend her territorial borders and their independence. You can see the same pathetic situation in this our country. Nigeria has become an object of joke and a subject of major headlines in world news. What a tragedy! Then, what are our warriors doing? Most of them are asleep like the warriors of General Saul Kish of Ancient Israel.

For the purpose of further enlightenment, let us see more striking features of a sleeping giant.

1. **They talk more and act less.** When you come to any place and the people there do more talking than doing, then there is a high tendency they have more sleeping giants. This is because most giants are known for complaining rather than complementing. They complain about almost everything that is absent in the land, but do nothing to put things on ground. They complain there is poverty but would not help in alleviating the suffering of the poor ones around them.

They wail on top of their voices about the crisis in the economy, polity and religious spheres, but they would never initiate or support platforms for resolving those crisis. These people claim to love their country and also might cry out in time of national disaster or disorder. However, they would not go further to proffer concrete solutions even when they have all or most of the resources required to bring about solution.

Apostle James said, ***"For instance, you come upon an old friend dressed in rags and half-starved and say, 'Good morning, friend! Be clothed in Christ! Be filled with the Holy Spirit!' and walk off without providing so much as a coat or a cup of soup – where does that get you? Isn't it obvious that God-talk without God-act is outrageous nonsense?"*** (2:16-17 TM). So, when you see people who have what it takes to end hunger in the land but they choose to revel in their own state of surplus while the land moans in scarcity and famine, such people are the sleeping giants.

If you know any institution whose heads or leaders are satisfied with identifying loopholes in their corporate systems without doing the needful to address the problems, then, they have simply identified themselves as sleeping giants. These kinds of people are unbelievably lazy not because they are not busy, but because they are busy doing the wrong things, and not busy about the right and proper things – the most pressing issues. So, they talk a good line but tow a bad line.

They shout out what they see is the problem and go back to sleep shortly after that. They issue press conferences and that is all to it – no further actions! They report that the economy is failing or that the national currency is depreciating in value compared to other currencies, but crawl back into their bed to continue their sleep. Those who are not well-informed about their track-record of whistle-blowing without action fall gullible to their pseudo report. Sleeping giants do more talking than action. Too bad for the giant of Africa!

2. **They are busy yet guilty.** Like I mentioned few lines earlier, they are lazy not because they are not doing anything but because they are doing the improper things. This is what I prefer to describe as busy yet guilty. Being busy is good, at least, for the exercise of the mind and body. But business without accomplishment brings frustration. There is a passage in Bible history to describe this point and highlight the result that follows.

First Kings Chapter twenty, verses thirty-nine through forty states: ***"As the king passed by, he cried unto the king: and he said, Thy servant went out into the midst*** *of the battle; and, behold, a man turned aside, and brought a man unto me, and said, Keep this man: if by any means he be missing, then shall thy life be for his life, or else thou shalt pay a talent of silver. And as thy servant was busy here and there, he was gone. And the king of Israel said unto him, so shall thy judgement be, thyself hast decided it."* Looking at this incident, you can see why most people are entangled in the web of self-imposed suffering and frustration.

Every man or nation is facing tough situations all over the world. No individual or nation is immune against tension either from within their borders or from outside. But to contain these disruptions needs focus on major issues that can bring safety, economic surplus, and reduce suffering when properly and adequately addressed. Times of war or tension are not fun times or party times. Unfortunately, most people see the opposite because they are short-sighted. And the others who see it the way it is often allow the tension to overwhelm them to the point of not recognizing the opportunities to stand up and be counted for great accomplishments.

Yet a good number of others only see opportunities for self-enrichment like the war against insurgency and terrorism in Nigeria. Men who are supposed, nay empowered by law to fight terrorism, guard the sovereignty of the nation and achieve lasting peace and tranquillity, are daily alleged to have compromised the code of their calling because of selfish gains. News reports tell us they are engaging the terrorists in combat to rid them out, but the result of their engagement is nothing to write home about.

Imagine a land where nomads are freely wielding AK-47 rifles in the noon, having a filled day killing, raping women and maiming innocent people as well as sacking them from their ancestral homes. Imagine in the same land where the military and other security paraphernalia – giants in their own right – go on holiday and always claiming to be on top of the ugly situation. Now, what shall we say or conclude about such giants?

What shall we say of the executives who convene every mid-week only to rise from their sittings to be confronted with the brazen result of executive lawlessness, laziness and lukewarmness? What shall we say or conclude of men who man our borders with other countries? They watch riffraff and some "Gadhafi-trained-terrorists" as recently revealed by Mr President, Muhammad Buhari move in and out of the God-blessed giant of Africa. Are these men awake and alive to their core responsibilities or simply busy here and there as affirmed by the Holy Scriptures quoted earlier?

Take a second but closer look at that piece of history as captured by the author of the Book of Kings. It was in a time of battle; war was on and an important assignment was entrusted to him. The consequence of failing in the assignment was also stated to him, which means that he was well aware of the stakes. But he became entangled in other matters which he perhaps, believed to deserve his attention too. Then, he lost focus.

What was he doing? He confessed that he was busy here and there. Did he accomplish anything of noble worth in his new-found, self-allotted task? Not any that he was bold or proud to mention. Instead of achieving something to be proud of, he lost something that he would be punished for. That is often the story of sleeping giants. This is a story they need in order to change without delay otherwise they will end in regret for being busy yet guilty.

3. **They are complacent.** Another woeful and worrisome feature of sleeping giants is that they revel in complacency. This is a state of having a feeling of contentment, quiet pleasure or satisfaction with oneself. It is a feeling that usually ruminate the heart of those who presume they have

done so much that they need to take a break. But one thing they fail to realize is that dwelling on past glories make them become irrelevant, insignificant and then lose touch with current realities. And when calamity strikes, it sweeps them away along with the rest. These people run the risk of becoming irrelevant which pushes them into a state of eventual, perpetual sleep.

Bible history is replete with stories of giants who became complacent and lost out in the scheme of things in their countries. Some of them were disrobed of honour and wealth while few others messed their leadership grace. Still a good number of others who never rose to prominence in life can be found in our most reliable history book – the Holy Bible. One of such men was President David Jesse of Israel.

In a time of war to possess the country of Ammon; in a time kings (giants) lead their men to war, the Commander in Chief of the army of Israel became complacent and remained at the presidential quarters. What was he doing there? History has the record.

"And it came to pass in an eveningtide, that David arose from off his bed, and walked upon the roof of the king's house; and from the roof he saw a woman washing herself; and the woman was very beautiful to look upon" (2 Samuel 11:2). Did you see that? His

Excellency, a giant, was sleeping late in the afternoon. And when he awoke, he went on a leisurely walk on the roof of the presidential villa. From there, another sight caught his attention. Then, what did he further do?

"And David sent and enquired after the woman. And one said, Is not this Bathsheba, the daughter of Eliam, the wife of Uriah the Hittite? And David sent messengers, and took her; and she came in unto him, and he lay with her; for she was purified from her uncleanness: and she returned unto her house" (vss. 3-4). Did you see His Excellency's giant stride? Awake O sleeper!

Recently, some terrorists masquerading as herdsmen invaded some communities in Benue State, Nigeria, and other neighbouring states in the North Central part of the country. The killings were too many that they sparked off a nationwide condemnation from all well-meaning citizens. Our Number One citizen gave orders to the Inspector General of Police at the time to move his office and command to the troubled state of Benue and forestall further mayhem. But that order was blatantly rebuffed and disobeyed, and the murderous killing by those herdsmen continued to split the country. That was exactly what David did.

Whatever reasons the police chief had were not enough to treat his superior's orders with a jaunty wave of the hand as it were. And about a month later, Mr President who gave the order found out his order was not complied with. What did he do as the Chief Security Officer of the nation? He brought it to the knowledge of the citizens and the whole world. That was all! And the mockery of the executive continued across the globe. This is what I describe as executive lawlessness! Complacency of the highest order! Outrageous nonsense, which must stop in the giant of Africa!

4. **They make excuses for their docility.** This is one of the issues trending among our leaders in this dispensation of Change. While campaigning for the general elections of 2015, some people ganged up and came up with the Change Mantra which finally got them into power at the federal government.

During those days and prior to the elections, they had boasted how they would fix electricity in six months, banish corruption from the country to only God-knows-where, and create millions of jobs in their first year. This is 2018. Many companies have closed down and employees became jobless. One US Dollar that was exchanging for N195 when they assumed office began to sell at almost N500 official rate! And it stayed at that rate for quite some time. Terrorism increased with the resurgence of the so-called Fulani herdsmen.

Boko Haram that was said to be "technically defeated" in 2016 – a year after they took over – resurfaced in a more deadly way and kidnapped school girls in Dapchi town in the Northern part of the country. This incident was a total bizarre to many Nigerians; a case of the more you look, the less you see.

What's more? Cost of food stuffs went high with a bag of rice higher in price than when they took over. Petrol price was raised from N97 to N145, the highest we have seen since after the military regime. All these things attest to the fact that the giants who vigorously campaigned and wooed Nigerians for change in government went to sleep shortly after clinching the mandate. If not, why did it take them six whole months to appoint the federal ministers who they believed would make the change possible? And when confronted with the obvious, they began to make excuses.

First and majorly, they claimed that the immediate past government that was led by Dr Goodluck Jonathan wasted every kobo and destroyed the economy. They said this while campaigning and promised to fix it when they come on board. I then wonder why the noise about the past governments' excesses when they already claimed so and promised to do better.

Another excuse is that the oil price hit an all-time low when they took off so no much money to bring about the change they promised. Meanwhile, the International Monetary Fund (IMF) managers warned the Nigerian government of the possibility of low oil prices and consequent recession, yet they did not heed the caution. What about the billions of naira removed from looters of our treasury?

At a time in 2017, about 322 million dollars Abacha loot was returned by the Switzerland government. At other times, millions and billions were recovered from within. Why were they still crying wolf of wasted economy under previous leaders? If it was not Jonathan, they blamed the political party he emerged on as president. If not the political party, they blamed the fall in oil prices. If not the oil prices, they said that corruption was fighting back. That has been the latest song on the deceitful lips of our change campaigners. These things are what happen when giants are asleep in a country.

As I write, the herdsmen-turned-terrorists have continued to invade communities and villages in the North-Central part of the country while the Boko Haram maintained their suicide bombings in the North

East. They say our security chiefs and their forces are working round the clock to quell nationwide violence, yet these murderous minds are having their way with no serious arrests so far recorded, no prosecution nor conviction. No one has gone to jail. You ask them why. The security forces blame it on the justice system, I mean, the judiciary.

Turn to the judiciary and hear their excuse: It is the fault of the justices of the high or appeal courts, or the failure of the prosecution panel to come up with concrete evidence. At the end, the cases are thrown out for lack of merit or whatever nomenclature that pleases his Lordship to use. The accused person returns to "his business" for which some highly placed persons in the state or nation are paying handsomely. The cycle of blame continues and the nation continues to waste. Too bad!

When we see people especially those in leadership positions across the country – community, constituency or at the centre – exhibit these traits do not look any further; they are sleeping giants. They may have their reasons for complaining and doing nothing to help. They may have reasons for being busy about the non-issues or being complacent in the middle of national crisis. They may have reasons for their excuses which may appear cogent. Yet, sleeping when they are needed to use their natural endowments to contribute to sustainable development is not acceptable in any wise.

They are giants, no doubts, and giants volunteer to take on the challenge one on one. They do not make excuses or go to bed when duty calls or when responsibility beckons. Notwithstanding, we shall now proceed to look at why these giants are sleeping. We will also give them reasons why they should be awake and equally make them see what would happen when they awake.

WHY GIANTS ARE ASLEEP

The question must be asked: Why are the giants asleep? Why have men and women with ideas to transform the system gone to sleep? What actually happened to their conscience and sense of goodwill? Or is it a case where they no longer think with their minds? These questions and more shall be answered in this next point. We will find out why they have refused to or are taking all eternity to get up from the bed of excuses, idleness and complacency. So, why are these great minds not awake?

1. It is because **sleep is a natural thing** that is capable or that has the power to keep a man in bed longer than necessary. Sleep is a natural phenomenon, no doubt, and everyone sleeps – agreed. Apart from

the response to nature, there are other reasons why people sleep, even in inordinate times. When an activity is not interesting or fascinating, people get bored and the next thing that usually follows boredom is sleep.

Imagine in a meeting where issues that are being discussed do not elicit deep interest or arouse tense emotions that can stir up contributions, the participants either walk out or fall asleep. Imagine in a class where the teacher is not communicating well to arouse the interest or rapt attention of the students, they seem to flow with the tendency to sleep off. Just imagine that. Now bring it to our collective existence as a community, constituency or country.

When governance is not all-embracing and all-inclusive, most people get bored and go to sleep. When only a few men who think or believe they have all the answers in a supposed participatory democracy shut others out, people easily choose the path of sleeping in their corner. When national mandate becomes a family business or is turned into a political party mandate, others feel marginalized and can go to sleep. When people with sharpened skills and intelligent minds are side-lined, while those who have lost sparkle and touch of current realities and strategies for developing the public or private sector are engaged, people lose interest and may soon go to sleep.

A country like ours where the exodus of core professionals in essential services is on the rise, most people who cannot afford to join the train get fed up and resort to sleeping. If they protest to be given the opportunity to make things happen in the land instead of keeping quiet and mute, they have little or no hope of success. So, to go to sleep becomes the inevitable option as it were. An unpalatable sorry situation, I must say.

2. Another reason people go to sleep is **apathy**. This is a condition where it is believed that nothing will ever change if they act. As it was in the beginning, so shall it continue forever becomes their poplar slogan. And this is a dangerous spirit. Apathy makes people become docile – a state of inactivity and unwillingness to do something to solve a problem. Most of the people who could bring respite and solution to challenges in the nation have resigned to a life of watching from the sides, being afflicted by this dangerous lukewarm spirit.

A lukewarm spirit makes potential world-changers become confused of which side of the divide to pitch tent with. When they look at trending with its attendant fanfare, hyped media advertisement, and large following, they get the feeling that the minority good team cannot win the game. They see and know that the trending and its large following mean no good for the nation; that the few good men on the minority team may not be able to rise let alone be heard in the land. So, they quit trying to see reasons to keep pushing forward with the few relentless good men since it looks obvious to them that they have no chance of turning the tide. This plays out in almost all sectors of our collective existence thus throwing more and more people into a state of slumber.

To reverse this ugly trend, the few good men must settle in their minds not to give up no matter their slim chances at winning. If we probe into history, we will find and discover that time is what separates champion from cowards. With time, a few more good men will begin to realize the subtle harm their membership of the popular party has done to the general good and they will begin to decamp from there.

Whatever be the case, apathy is like a secret agent or spy in the camp of the good men that cripples their willingness and resolve to awake to their responsibilities. We must do all we can to avoid getting infected by the spirit of apathy. It makes many a giant to become indifferent to the need of the society and incapacitates them so they can no longer awake and act.

3. Another reason people give up and go to sleep is when they feel they have **nothing at stake**. Most of our people feel they have nothing to lose if the economy is down or if the political landscape is eroded. They do not see themselves incurring any loss so they go into slumber. This is what we call I-do-not-care attitude.

Some of them may feel that they have everything they need to live comfortable lives so do not see the point meddling in state or national affairs that could hardly be solved to benefit them. Since they have decided to sleep, they also let the sleeping dogs or dead horses to lie. The elites are the most culpable in this regard.

They are educated, have secured jobs and employments with very good salary packages, and access to hard loans from their employers. Some of them have their children schooling abroad while others who want their children around in the country, put them in the best and expensive schools. They have the privilege of enjoying holidays outside the country and they also can afford the best services in the land.

They become like the proverbial rich farmer in the Book of Luke 12:15-21, who gathered enough just for himself and cared less of others. Our people say that it is someone who has not encountered serious challenges or problems that does not care about other people who are going through problems. If it happened to you, you would feel for those it is happening to right now.

One major problem with this attitude is that it easily creates a division between these elites and the other common people who bear the brunt of their negligence. Since the elites are considered as people with the required leverage to speak for the masses but fail to do so for the reason earlier stated, a gulf between the two camps is readily formed. When those who hold sway in the country, mostly the politicians see this, they leverage on it to further divide the people along many lines – tribe, religion, ethnicity, education, etc. This is the major reason the elites and the commons seem not to ever come to a point of agreement.

Since the elites feel they have nothing to lose in the current equation; with the belief that any fight they put up with those holding the country to ransom will largely benefit the masses, they back out and crawl into their shell of I-do-not-care life. Even when they know that the politicians love it so, and that it is destroying the country, they seem to be under that charm and never wish to be free from its negative influence.

But in recent times, as our country prepares for the 2019 general elections, hope seems to be rising for all as some of these elites have started waking up from their sleep. I will discuss this development in my closing chapter.

4. Most giants go to sleep for a different reason than the three I have briefly highlighted so far. One other reason is **over-confidence**. What do I mean by this? The following scripture passage, nay, piece of Biblical history will help us understand it better. ***"The Master sent a message against Jacob. It landed right on Israel's doorstep. All the people soon heard the message, Ephraim and the citizens of Samaria. But they were a proud and arrogant bunch. They dismissed the message, saying, "Things aren't that bad. We can handle anything that comes. If our buildings are knocked down, we'll rebuild them bigger and finer. If our forests are cut down, we'll replant them with finer trees"*** (Isaiah 9:8-10 TM).

Can you see any correlation with our case in the country? When there is a call for giants to awake, we should know that there is problem in the land that needs to be fixed, and that these giants are being expected to do the fixing. But when these giants begin to see the problem or challenge as nothing compared to what their ability or capability can handle, then they tend to remain in their slumbering state much longer. This is what over-confidence can do.

It is good for people to know what they can handle. However, over-estimation of one's ability in relation to the challenge at hand is arrogance and an announcement of self-importance. A call for duty is such that requires prompt action. This is because when duty calls and responsibility beckons and there is no prompt or proportionate response, the task accumulates over time.

When this happens, the tendency for it to become over-whelming and arduous gets higher. Thus, a little work if neglected for so long can become a big deal. Just like a little sin when allowed destroys the soul, a little task when overlooked becomes a monstrous challenge. The cause of this negligence often times is over-confidence – the presumption of "we can handle what comes".

The economy is nose-diving; while the economists are worried by the ugly trend, the government are saying it is no big deal until the nation slides into an economic recession. The polity is over-heated and the politicians say, it is okay and carry on with politicking until party supporters start clashing and killing one another. Terrorists are attacking and sacking villages, and the security operatives say they are just communal misunderstanding and clashes until a Boko Haram is formed. Criminal elements among the security forces harassing innocent citizens, the security chiefs deny they are their men or that they are unemployed youths showing their angst.

People are hungry in the land and the leaders keep quiet until armed robbery, kidnapping and ritual killing become their lifestyle. There is mass misappropriation of public funds by government officials and political office holders, and the citizens' cries are neglected until protests and agitations hit the country from North to South, and East to West. When will our people begin to learn from history?

There are clear signals of increased crime rate, poverty level, human trafficking, financial corruption, and systems collapse, yet those with the mandate to wade in and avert them are saying that there is no cause for alarm – *"We can handle whatever comes."* You could not adequately keep our borders from being hacked by unscrupulous riff raff from neighbouring countries, yet you say that you can stop them from unleashing mayhem on Nigerians. You could not block loopholes in the civil service through which civil servants siphon money, yet you want to fight corruption.

You could not build schools for our teaming children across the country, now they are out on the streets; you want to pay them monthly stipends – what is it for? You could not build good, well-equipped hospitals, yet you are boasting that you can handle the outbreak of cholera, Ebola and other life-threatening and life-terminating diseases. Our airports could not make the list of best 100 airports in the world, and not among the best in Africa, yet you boast of being able to prevent infiltrations of hard drugs into the supposedly giant of Africa.

God sent a warning message to Judah and Israel which should awaken all sleeping giants and move them to act fast, yet they dismissed it with a jaunty wave of the hand – it is nothing! International Monetary Fund (IMF) sent a warning to Nigeria that we should be careful with our borrowing trend and tendencies, yet our leaders shoved it aside and said, we can handle it.

Prophet Jeremiah recorded God's message and sent it to the people, but their leaders concluded it was no big deal: **"Things aren't that bad. We can handle anything that comes. If our buildings are knocked down, we'll rebuild them bigger and finer. If our forests are cut down, we'll replant them with finer trees."**

Did you see how over-confident and arrogant these people are? Just like some of ours – they feel that the trouble in the land is not enough to lose sleep. They say, it has not come to that. If the oil prices drop so low that we cannot get enough to fund our annual budget, we run to IMF and the Paris Club to loan us some money.

If our refineries are shut down and not working, we ship our crude overseas and get them refined. It does not matter how much it cost, our citizens do not protest over such profligacy and *prodigalism*; they will pay for it even if it costs a fortune to afford fuel products.

If our schools and education sector remain dysfunctional, we will send our children to Ghana, Rwanda, South Africa, Europe and America to study there. After all, we will not kill ourselves over dysfunctional educational sector – we met it like that when we assumed office. These are what sleeping giants, out of over-confidence, are saying in response to the clarion call to rescue the land.

They, sometimes, use press briefings, sponsored advertorials, and televised broadcast to tell the citizens that the economy is not as recessive as it is being screamed on pages of newspapers. That the menace of terrorists who parade towns and cities killing and destroying lives and property is not as bad as is being revealed by international press or other agencies such as Amnesty International. They deny these agencies' report on the violation of human rights by government security apparatus, and claim they are investigating the report. At the end of the day, no one gets to hear or know about their findings.

The killing by herdsmen continues. Terrorists who have been "technically defeated" raise their game of destruction to the next level. The citizens continue to wail and groan under worse economic conditions with no money, no food, and no defence of their fundamental rights. Why all these? The giants who should wake up at the alert of danger, under-estimate the situation by concluding that the threats are no big deal.

They feel that it is not as bad as being projected. They tell all that care to listen that they are on top of the situation when in truth, they are under it sleeping. The bomb that will awaken them so suddenly is ticking and will soon go off. I only fear the outcome and pray that the righteous ones will be saved.

WHY SLEEPING GIANTS MUST AWAKE

Our people say that whatever time of the day a man awakes is morning to him. Howbeit, the sleeper may not recover easily. This is why it is imperative to do the permutations and calculations before allowing oneself be thrown into a state of slumber or eventual sleep. Time spent in sleeping is not recovered by saying that anytime a man wakes up is his morning unless he begins to do what he should have done from the moment he awakes even if it is in the midnight.

Most people have been deceived by similar proverbs, adage or slogans such as "Life begins at forty", etc. so, they stay idle, single, unemployed or even live prodigal lives waiting to reach the age of forty before thinking of how to begin to pursue a worthy cause or purposeful life. It took Nigeria almost forty years from 1960 to embrace the almighty democracy in 1999!

Yet, nineteen years after, our helmsmen are still experimenting with it to the detriment of the lives of the citizens. One begins to wonder when they would leave the laboratory of experiment to the field of expedition. This move or transition is very crucial that all who have been sleeping on duty or off duty must awake now.

The need for men and women to awake from their sleep mode and become responsible and responsive to the need of the hour in their respective domains cannot be over-flogged. We have said much about why people get carried away, doze off and forget they are being expected by others to take the lead in national development. Now, let us see some reasons why they should, as a matter of urgency, do so.

1. The epistle of Apostle Paul to the Romans scores some points in this regard. ***"And that, knowing the time, that now it is high time to awake out of sleep,..."*** (vs. 11). One reason to be awake is that **it is high time to do so**. The Word of God which is the submission of Heaven has given us one good reason to wake up. Heaven has observed the activities in the land, probed the works of men – the leaders and the led alike – and came out with the conclusion that it is high time we awake from sleep.

God, by the decrees of His Parliament in Heaven, created times and seasons. In President Solomon's Book of Ecclesiastes chapter three, the wisest national leader wrote that there is time for everything and a season for every event. There is a time to shout and a time to keep quiet. There is also a time to sleep and a time to awake from sleep. God created time to sleep. And I dare say that Nigeria has done enough sleeping, it is time to awake.

We cannot continue to sleep when it is quite clear that sleeping time is over. The presidency, the legislatures, the judiciary, the private organizations, the civil service and all other corporate as well as individual entities in this God-blessed country must note that they have done well sleeping. Now, it is time to awake out of sleep.

Do not argue about this, saying, Pastor Chris, you do not know what you are talking about: we have not been sleeping. We are well awake and working. Well, I am not the only one who observed that you are sleeping. God and His Parliament first made the observation and then used one of their spokespersons, Paul, to write it down that you have been asleep and that it is high time you awoke from sleep. And you know what, God cannot tell a lie! Whatever He observes and chronicles in His Book is always true and most reliable. No one can contest it.

But, come to think of it, do you argue or contest with facts? The confirmation of that observation is clearly evident in the country – everywhere you look. The rot and robbery of justice in the judiciary, the nonchalance in the civil service, the irresponsibility of the legislature, and the impunity among the executives – all attest to Heaven's position on the fact that the national, state and local authorities have been sleeping and must awake now. The rising cost of basic food commodities, and the unrestrained inflation are key indicators that the key leaders have either been sleeping or slumbering on their seats.

The oppression of the poor in the society and the glorification of godless godfathers also point to the brazen fact that men who should maintain equity are all asleep. So, these people must awake from sleep in quick response to Heaven's call. Even the other citizens who are not privileged to be in the leadership of the state cannot claim to be any better – they are also culpable in this regard. This is because all available evidence point to the fact that they are guilty as well.

The degree of docility and apathy exhibited by these citizens both the elite class and the masses is very alarming. We have so much energy to change the ugly status, yet we only find the pleasure of exerting and dissipating it on social media and other less relevant platforms.

Voicing our displeasure on social media and doing nothing further to enforce our positions mean we are yet to awake out of sleep. Generating heat in the news with our cries for change but never making the principals feel the heat indicate we are not yet awake to reality and how things work. The time has come to do so. Now is the time to heed God's recommendation, nay, command to awake. And we must be serious about it.

2.   Why must sleeping giants awake? It is because **our salvation is nearer** than when we first believed.

What this means is that our nation is about to experience deliverance from captivity and oppression in the hands of oppressors. It means that the time of our emancipation is around the corner.

The epistle of Apostle Paul noted, ***"The night is far gone, the day of his return will soon be here"*** (vs. 12 TLB). Actually, this talks about the return of Jesus Christ the Saviour of mankind to the earth. However, I want us to note that God's visitation comes to every nation in different forms so one must be awake. Time of such visitations brings deliverance, blessing, etc. Thus, some people who are not awake do not usually know when God visits them with salvation.

The Holy Bible history captured one of such scenarios in the Gospel book of Luke chapter nineteen from verse thirty-six to verse forty-four. It reads:

"Then the crowds spread out their robes along the road ahead of him, and as they reached the place... the whole procession began to shout and sing as they walked along, praising God for all the wonderful miracles Jesus had done. "God has given us a King!"..."Long live the King!" let all heaven rejoice! Glory to God in the highest heavens...But as they came closer to Jerusalem (or Abuja, Nigeria or any community) *and he saw the city ahead, he began to cry, "Eternal peace was within your reach and you turned it* *down," he wept, "and now it is too late…"* (TLB) Emphasis mine

One prayer I must pray for Nigeria before I move on is this: May it not be too late for us to awake and embrace eternal peace and joy from God in Jesus name – Amen!

Just look at that! The people of Jerusalem were not awake to realise God was visiting them with "eternal peace". The Amplified Version of the Holy Bible says it plainer: **"And as He approached, He saw the city, and He wept [audibly] over it, exclaiming, Would that you had known personally, even at least in this your day, the things that make for peace (for freedom from all the distresses that are experienced as the result of sin and upon which your peace – your security, safety, prosperity, and happiness – depends)! But now they are hidden from your eyes"** (vs. 41-42).

They did not know the day of their salvation so they missed it. The people were caught up in other businesses as usual and so did not recognize that the salvation – freedom from all oppression they had prayed so long for was around the corner. This can only happen when a people are asleep and not awake.

We must not be like the people of Jerusalem. Today, most countries of the world do not recognize Jerusalem as God once recognized it. Just recently, the nation of Israel celebrated her 70th independence anniversary and the American strong man, President Donald Trump recognized Jerusalem as the official capital of Israel. It was like the burst of a bubble. When he then moved the American embassy to Jerusalem with the whole world watching, history was made as prophecy was fulfilled. Yet, the entire world went gaga as a result of that bold move.

But the real question is: Would it have been like that if Jerusalem had been awake and accepted Christ as recorded by Luke the Apostle. If they had known their time of visitation and embraced the King of kings at that time, I bet, it would have been different. History repeats itself but Nigerians should not fall on the wrong side of history.

Zacchaeus was a man of the society who had all the political connections and economic muscle. He had the same opportunity that Jerusalem had but unlike the city that rejected the opportunity, Zacchaeus embraced his. In the same chapter of Luke 19 from verse one; Jesus was just passing through Jericho when Zacchaeus heard the news. Unlike the people of Jerusalem who continued with business as usual, he went out to see the King who had come to seek and save the world. This man was awake indeed. He went to a lot of trouble; went out of his way to get a glimpse of the Saviour.

And when Jesus saw how interested he was in knowing Him, He paid him an unscheduled visit. *"Meanwhile, Zacchaeus stood before the Lord and said, "Sir, from now on I will give half my wealth to the poor, and if I find I have overcharged anyone on his taxes, I will penalize myself by giving him back four times as much!" Jesus told him, "This means that salvation has come to this home today…"* (Luke 19:8-9 TLB).

Fellow Nigerians, we must awake now because our salvation is nearer than when we first began to expect it. When you plant or cultivate a farmland, you naturally expect harvest. You do not sit idle and do nothing while expecting a good and rich harvest; you still work the farm. You weed it, dress the crops and use insecticide or pesticide where necessary to keep pests away. Until harvest time, you do not sleep over your cultivated farm land.

The same applies to a country and to our individual situations. There is need to continue to strengthen the economy until a rich harvest is ready for us all. Because the time of our salvation is nearer than when we first started the march to political and economic freedom, we must not rest on our oars, but must be awake to see to it.

God created the entire heavens and the earth in just six days and then rested on the seventh day. That rest was actually a natural break, not an eternal one. God did not go to sleep; He only observed a day's rest. He neither slumbers nor sleeps (Psalm 121). So, what has He been doing ever since then? He has been working to ensure our safety, prosperity and peace. But in all these, He wants to always work with us and through us.

He did the work of creation alone as the Triune God with the Trinity in Council. Now, He wants to work with us and through us to make the world He created be filled with love, peace, joy and prosperity. But most of us, unfortunately, are not responding because we are sleeping when we should be alert on duty.

Imagine if God takes a nap or dozes off for a minute, nay, for a second or nanosecond, the entire world systems would collapse and the universe would be in unimaginable chaos. We take a nap from time to time because we are humans. That is quite understandable. But sleeping when we should be awake becomes an abuse of nature. Now is the time to cut that abuse and be awake.

Heaven is about to grant us the salvation – freedom, economic recovery, political stability and tribal harmony – we have been crying for. Let us not continue to be asleep and miss out on this supernatural and divine appointment. We must be awake to be part of the process.

3.   Another reason to awake according to our text is that the night is far spent, or according to The Message Version: **"The night is about over, dawn is about to break" (vs. 12).** The Psalm of David says that **"weeping may endure for a night, but joy comes in the morning"** (30:5). Anyone who has expectations of joy at the break of dawn does not sleep away like those who have no hope or expectation.

Like I noted earlier, that a man who sleeps and snores away usually does not know what goes on in the night. Such a man runs the risk of being attacked and overrun by robbers in the night. The enemy could break into his domain and take away his property. Night time is such a precarious time that even brave men fear to sleep and snore way. Sudden disaster usually comes when men are not really prepared. So is the case with night time because people sleep. But we have good news – night time is over!

In one of His famous parables, Jesus Christ narrated that a man planted good crops and went to sleep. While he was asleep at night, his enemy came and planted bad crops among the good ones he had planted in the day time. Enemies do not like to be exposed so they crawl around in the night – figuratively speaking, at unexpected, odd times – to do their evil work. A man who is surrounded by such enemies do not sleep away in order to stay safe and keep his home safe, too. So, you can see that night time is a very difficult time. But now, the night is over, Nigeria, let us do the needful while it is dawn.

If you live in Lagos or had lived in Lagos, Nigeria, you would appreciate the need to awake on time and not to sleep away. Many people who work far from their homes do not need sermon to wake up on time to prepare and leave for work. For some who live in places like Ikorodu or Badagry but work on the Island, that is, Victoria Island, Lekki or Ikoyi, they know that for them to be at their places of work on time, they must get up from bed by 3am or 4am and leave within the hour. If they do not do so, the heavy traffic on Lagos routes especially routes to the Island would hold them three to four hours and make them late to work.

Now, that is not fun at all. However, it is their sacrifice to keep their jobs. The same applies to everything else that concerns us as a people in a country. If we must preserve the future, we must be awake on time to our responsibilities. It is the sacrifice at the present in order to enjoy the future.

Why is our nation in turmoil? Why are the people suffering in a land full of surplus wealth? Why did a brief time of recession launch us into untold hardship? It is because the leadership did not realize that early to bed is early to rise. That nursery rhyme still has a profound message to teach us. "Early to bed, early to rise; makes a man healthy, wealthy and wise". Our leaders partied all night such that they went to bed very late – almost at the break of dawn. Now, to awake at the break of dawn has become a Herculean task for them. Wise President Solomon remarked, ***"Unlucky the land whose king is a young pup, and whose princes*** (leaders) ***party all night…"*** (Ecclesiastes 10:16 TM Emphasis mine).

Recession is only a natural occurrence because there are seasons for everything under heaven. There is a season to laugh and a season to cry. Recession is only a season of dwindling fortunes, a famine in Biblical term. But we were not prepared for it. Someone also said that recession is a time when money locates its original owners. That is, in my opinion, those who worked for money attract it during recession.

Our leaders were throwing parties, sharing state funds instead of saving and investing them. Thus, they threw our country into undeserved slavery. The citizens also were busy enjoying the spree, not realizing it was at the detriment of their future. Suddenly, disaster came knocking without warning because all played deaf and dumb in the drama. But there is hope.

Our reliable history record says so and we must believe it. We must get out of bed because the night of partying is over; the morning of productive living is here. The night of prodigalism is over; the dawn of progress is upon us. It is the dawn of a new era that is about to break upon us and we must be ready to embrace it. It is time to face the business of the day and redeem our nation from this horrible nightmare and ridicule.

When day breaks, wise people go out to work; they get down to business. Wise decisions are made, practical actions are taken. Men and women of wisdom all over the world awake to tackle real issues in order to get their countries out of recession or ugly situations. Our case must not be a contrast. The night is far spent, the day is at hand. Awake, o sleeper!

4. Now that night is over and the day is here, anyone who is sleeping, over-slumbering or dozing is considered a lazy man or an enemy of the progress of the nation. God is doing something new in the country that all eyes should be open to see and appreciate it. The spiritual, economic, political and socio-cultural climates are fast changing, and we must awake to join in the action to sustain that change.

Since we have moved from night to day where everything is made open, every eye should be peeled for opportunities to contribute to the things that would bring us the joy that comes with the break of dawn. We must remember that President David Jesse said it that joy comes in the morning. To be honest, only those who awake with the break of dawn and are prepared to seize the available opportunities that produce factors responsible for joy and rejoicing truly enjoy.

When a nation loses track of what heaven is doing amongst the sons of men on earth, the people remain in darkness, still thinking it is night time. But when they realize that there has been a divinely programmed paradigm shift, the leaders and the led, corporate bodies, public and private institutions will key into the divine program and process for their blessedness.

WHAT HAPPENS WHEN THEY ARE AWAKE?

A number of positive things would happen if our giants awake from sleep. The following points are some of the developments that would be obviously noted in the country.

1. **End of Frivolity:**
   Our economy has been under severe siege for a long time. A lot of plundering and squandering have taken place from the time of our independence until now. Over fifty-seven years down the line, we still struggle with economic management in this era of increased knowledge and advanced technology enhanced by extra-sharpened skills. This is because our money managers became money-mongers.

The legislators became *legis*-looters. The judiciary also joined the bandwagon and became *judi*-sharing. The civil servants turned themselves into civil lords amassing stupendous, illegitimate wealth at the expense of our nation's development to benefit all. But when the sleepers awake and realize they are custodians and not consumers of the nation's treasury, these lootings and laundering will stop – bringing to a compulsory end the frivolity.

When men and women realize they were ordained to increase state revenues and not to diminish them, they become conscious of how imperative it has become to end this madness. How could we be rated the number one country in terms of economic growth on the continent of Africa, and yet be ranked amongst the poorest nations in the world? What an unholy solemnization! A very unjust classification, indeed! This is all a result of the wasteful handling of our collective wealth as a sovereign nation.

When the Ghanaian giants awoke from their sleep some years ago, a Jerry Rawlings amongst them took the bold step and led other like-minded compatriots in his gold-rich country to do the needful. That move ended an era, so to speak, of *prodigalism* and wantonness such as never happened in the history of the Gold Coast. Remember the result? Ghana was purged and her economy began to thrive. I pray that Nigerian giants should awake fast before our nation is plunged into total darkness and doom.

2. **Rapid Reduction in Tribal Conflicts and Killings:**

   The disturbing issue of communal clashes and tribal tensions that often lead to several killings across the country especially in the northern parts would be crucially addressed when sleeping dogs awake. You can imagine that in a country where state governors receive security votes year in, year out, and security agencies get heavy allocations; there is this alarming rate of insecurity of lives and property.

God Almighty makes it clear in His Word as captured by Bible history that we must not walk in strife and envying. But this can only happen when we awake from our I-do-not-care attitude and begin to feel the need to be one another's keeper.

What we have continued to witness in the country are cases where lazy tribesmen in some communities up North and down South descend on other peaceful neighbours – killing and destroying their property in utter defiance of our sovereign laws and statutory security bodies. In some cases, they plunder these communities without a blink of the eyes. These ugly developments often happen under the watch of the security apparatus of their respective states.

What happened recently in Kaduna State of Nigeria, for instance, was a result of envy, that led to hatred and then, killing of innocent people. Some people, I mean, those heartless murderers could not stand the peace and serenity that surrounded the Southern Kaduna. So, out of envy, as reliable sources allegedly reported, they went in and unleashed mayhem on the people while their government watched from the side lines.

People no longer value human lives in this part of the world that they, being sponsored by politicians and other wicked men in authority, go in and take it out at will. These killings happened because the watchmen were sleeping on duty while the wicked took the advantage to do evil. Now, God is calling them to awake, and when they do, there would be change – the real change that would bring these senseless killings to an end.

3. **When sleeping giants awake, the people will walk in honesty**.

Our text says, *"Let us walk honestly as in the day…"* This implies that men of honesty do not walk in darkness or behind closed doors. Their work is always in the open for all to see. Men who operate behind closed doors usually have hidden agenda which they do not wish for the public to know about. And because that is their style, they do not often care about others who are not like them.

Behind those closed doors, they cook up lies and call it diplomacy which they introduce into the system. But when men of good conscience who have been complacent begin to rise, integrity is restored in the system, truth begins to prevail, and honesty and transparency in the work place begin to thrive.

Jesus Christ had a problem with the leaders of His day. He saw that their ways were always shrouded in secrecy. So He confronted them thus: **"He that believeth on him is not condemned; but he that believeth not is condemned already, because he hath not believed in the name of the only begotten Son of God. And this is the condemnation, that light is come into the world, and men loved darkness rather than light, because their deeds are evil. For everyone that doeth evil hated the light, lest his deeds should be reproved. But he that doeth truth cometh to the light, that his deeds may be made manifest, that they are wrought in God"** (John 3:18-21).

Plainly speaking, evil men who operate in the night do not want good men to be awake and expose what they are doing. They wish everyone should go to sleep when they are working out their evil agenda. When they are done in the dark, they push out their work to their cronies who help them actualize it in the day.

And because the watchmen are asleep when they should be awake, they become ignorant of these wicked devices cooked up in the night which manifest in the day. But when these giants are awake and are watching at their duty post, men are careful to walk as plainly as they can, and this promotes honesty and transparency in the day.

4. **Giants awake to quell storms of life**.

There are seasons when storms rage and rock the boat of individuals, organizations or even the nation at large. This is a natural occurrence; nothing new or strange – no one is shielded or exempted from these times. But when men sleep, the storms can rock their boat and may sink it if they are not awake. This is why the great men in our national boat should be awake so that when storms arise, they can do the job which nature, God and humanity bestowed on them the privilege to do.

Jesus Christ was fast asleep in the boat conveying Him and His disciples across to the other side. Then, the storms began to roar and rage, hitting their boat and harassing the disciples who were awake. This scenario paints a picture of the fact that, when a nation is experiencing a compulsory transition to another level, some players of the polity or economy should not sleep nor spend all night sleeping even if they must sleep. It is never a moment to do so in order not to forget what is at stake. It is during such moments that the enemies of the state who do not want to see the success of that transition double their hustle to stop the process and thus, hold the nation to ransom.

But in response to the demands of nature, Jesus Christ who has all things figured out fell asleep. I bet if Jesus had not known the outcome of that journey, He would not have gone to sleep. No one really sleeps sound in the midst of storms. Jesus did because, He, being God, knew what would happen and what He was going to do. So, when the storms blew hot and hard against their boat and the disciples cried out, He awoke and first of all, calmed the storm before scolding them for being fearful. That is what giants do.

They rescue their people from perishing in the land. They get them out of dicey situations. They calm raging storms battering their national carrier. Jesus rescued His own people, but unfortunately in our clime, our own leaders, masters of men, often ignore their cry for rescue and sleep on. But if they awake and respond to the need of the hour, every storm in the nation would surely be calm. That is their responsibility.

5. **When sleeping giants awake, their lost identity will be restored.**

   When we read the story of the Prodigal Son as narrated by Jesus Christ Himself and chronicled by Doctor Luke in his letter to Most Honourable

Theophilus, we appreciate his courage to awake from slumber. This young man was born to be celebrated at home but he took his father's wealth and travelled to a far country and wasted it there on frivolous living.

This paints a similar picture of things that happen on our soil, in the country. Most of our political office holders or occupiers and their counterparts in ministries, departments and agencies of the governments across the land are guilty of this heinous criminal act. They launder our treasury to foreign lands and squander it on selfish and often prodigal living.

But back home, the people who are supposed to enjoy the wealth languish in abject poverty and extreme hunger and lack. The prodigal son did that, and only prodigal leaders or citizens can do such outrageous nonsense. They rob the country of development while they use the collective patrimony of the people to develop those foreign lands where they launder the wealth to.

Now, to such men, the call is made to them to repent and return. Just as the prodigal son came to himself and awoke from his self-induced slumber and started the journey home to put things straight, all our people who have wasted so much of our resources at national, state, and local levels are expected to do same without further hesitation.

History captured that the prodigal son realized he had lost his identity as a son to his father such that all he could ask for was to be taken back as a hired servant. There are so many of my countrymen who are afraid to follow the prodigal son's example because they do not believe they can be forgiven and restored. Now, such people are encouraged to awake from that deception as their sins would be forgiven and their lost identities as true Nigerians would also be restored.

The father of the prodigal son did not accept his son's request to be regarded as a hired servant. Instead, he pardoned him because of his repentance, and celebrated his home-coming. The same treatment awaits all sleepers who hear the voice of God and men calling them to awake today.

We cannot throw away the baby with the bath water as long as the baby has been washed clean. Those who have over the years painted our identity black ae hereby encouraged to make a clean-break of their atrocities. Let the runaway arise and come home and join hands in making our country the truly blessed land it was created to be.

We cannot continue to let them misrepresent us at any level. Our country and the African continent are more than what the outside world think of us irrespective of the several abuses some of our people attract to us. We must protect our collective identity as the giant of Africa and the pride of the whole world. Let all sleeping giants awake!

CHAPTER TWO

ARISE, O COMPATRIOT!

Nigeria's National Anthem – our national song and rhythm is calling on all citizens to arise: "Arise O Compatriot, Nigeria's call, obey…" We have seen in Chapter One how that many are sleeping, why they are sleeping and the urgent need for them to awake from their sleep. We have also explored the reasons why all giants at all levels must awake and the benefits of their waking up.

Now, let us look further into the next command from the God of creation who has given the command to awake. Remember, if this nation must get to the Promised Land of all-sufficiency and all-round prosperity, we must take His commands seriously. Otherwise, we will only awake to continue the things that have kept us in retardation and regrets.

The God of Creation through one of His spokesmen, Apostle Paul, is not only calling us to awake but also to arise. Like I noted earlier, it is possible for a country and her people to awake from sleep or slumber and yet remain in the bed of complacency, compromise and corruption. It is possible for the leaders and the rest of the citizens to open their eyes to the ills and anomalies going on in the country amongst their kith and kin, organizations and corporations, communities and council areas yet do nothing nor arise to the challenges of putting an end to those ills.

Just like a watchdog that awakens at the sensing of intrusion by an unfamiliar presence, and goes back to sleep without barking or getting up to confront it. What would you call such a dog? Would you call it a watchdog or an observer dog? Or you call it an action dog? Maybe we should adopt a better descriptive name for the people we call or refer to as the Watchdogs of the society. They have been watching but not working! So, I suggest we call them "Working Dogs" so they can live up to the name.

What I am saying here is that we must not only awake, but arise. In order to arise to obey the call and effectively respond to make this country better, we must arise from the dead. God has commanded: ***"…Awake, O sleeper, and arise from the dead, and Christ shall shine (make day dawn) upon you and give you light"*** (Ephesians 5:14 AMP). To understand this more, let us look at the following:

ARISE FROM THE DEAD

Who are the dead? Or what is being referred to as "the dead" in this scripture? I will like to bullet my perspectives as follows:

A. **Dead Souls:** In all honesty, there are dead people in every community. They are not physically dead, but spiritually dead. They are somehow emotionally or psychologically dead, too. They see things but cannot really comprehend them. They hear things but hardly understand them. They rarely feel the need of the hour because they are often self-consumed with dead thoughts. The god of this world has blinded them, pierced their hearts and consciences with hot iron, and mortified their senses so they cannot feel or sense any good.

They are dead souls though alive and look robustly healthy in the flesh. They have a name that they are alive but in the eyes of God, His Council and all godly people, they are dead. ***"And unto the angel of the church in Sardis write; These things saith he that hath the seven Spirits of God, and the seven stars; I know thy works, that thou hast a name that thou livest, and art dead."*** (Revelations 3:1).

The people in this church at Sardis had a name of people who were alive. Sardis was a city located at about 30 miles south of Thyatira and the capital of Lydia at that time. It was noted for its great wealth which among other trades came from its flourishing carpet industry. Here also were coins first mined.

These people were condemned by the Lord God for being wrongly motivated, insincere and hypocritical as well as being men pleasers. This can actually happen or be true of any nation and her people.

The people of Sodom and Gomorrah were dead but did not know it until fire came and devoured them. The generations that lived in Noah's time were dead men but they did not just realize it until the flood came on them. God warned Adam and Eve that the day they ate the forbidden fruit, they would die. They ate it, though they had breath in them, yet they were dead – cut off and disconnected from their Maker and Master, God.

It is common knowledge that wires could be joined together still and no current running through because the life (current-conducting) wire has been disconnected from the main power supply point. So, Adam and Eve were disconnected from the Source of their life. Hence, they heard the voice of God and ran into hiding. The voice that used to favour them began to frighten them. The presence of God that was supposed to bless them, banished them. This is what happens to a people who look lively but are really dead. Such men do not hear and what they hear do not make any good sense to them even as the dead do not hear anything.

But there are people who are among these dead men. They do not really and truly belong there but do not actually realize that they are among the dead, so they feel cosy and at home with them. They are truly alive but are walking with the dead. Why? It is because they do not see those people as dead people. They even support their cause and they benefit from them in some ways. So, to them, these folks are alive; they see themselves as equals or comrades – nothing to worry about.

But the One who knows all men is telling us that you are neither equals nor comrades. You are still alive – really and truly alive and living, but they are dead. **"Arise from the dead!"** is the command for you to hastily obey. Yes, you need to arise and get out from among them as fast as you can hear the command to arise.

In order to respond to the call to build one united nation under God, you have no option, nay, no better option than to arise from among dead men and women. They may be among the movers and shakers of the economy. They can only shake the economy, but cannot make it reflect on the commoners. They can only move the economy back and forth without moving the people's standard of living up an inch higher.

They have a name that they are alive but in essence, they are dead. And because dead people cannot make any meaningful impact other than exuding stomach-upsetting stench, these men cannot impact their communities or country positively. They are dead so get out from them! ***"Wherefore come out from among them, and be ye separate, saith the Lord… and I will receive you"*** (2 Corinthians 6:17). We cannot, but diligently obey this divine executive order.

B. **Dead Systems:** This is talking about organizations, governments, agencies, and organized structures. There are so many government and private organizations around us that are dead. Like dead people, they have a name that they are alive but are really dead. How do we identify them?

i. They support the cause of evil while claiming to be godly. They may have a form of godliness but deny the power of godliness in their day-to-day operations. If they are houses of assembly, they may begin their plenary with prayers but their true membership is in the club of Satan (Revelations 3:9 TM). If they are politicians, they may claim God the Father as their source, but in all honesty and fairness, they pledge and show allegiance to error-stricken mortals who go by the name, godfathers.

As government agencies or corporate organizations, they throw their weight behind flesh-inspired projects that preach worldliness and promote immorality. They are always ready to sponsor television programs that encourage the display of nudity, moral perversion and corruption.

A probe into the sustained broadcast or telecast of major reality shows across the country will reveal that big corporations and blue-chip companies are solidly behind them. They offer mouth-watering, soul-tempting and mind-blowing sums of money and other gifts to the winners and participants of these shows but would never donate a kobo to soul-lifting, godly programmes that can change the misfortune of the nation. These corporations are dead even though they appear to be making some so-called celebrities.

If you check very well, the ones who eventually become their brand ambassadors are oftentimes as dead as themselves. And God is saying to those who are not yet dead to arise from among them so the nation can truly become alive and well.

ii. In discussing the next point under dead systems, let us look at a scenario in Bible history that actually caught my attention. It is not a case of a dead government, but a very old one, which, in my submission is as good as dead. The record can be found in the book of First Kings chapter one and from verse one to verse ten. Let us see it:

"Now king David was old and stricken in years; and they covered him with clothes, but he gat no heat. Wherefore his servants said unto him, Let there be sought for my lord the king a young virgin: and let her stand before the king, and let her cherish him, and let her lie in thy bosom, that my lord the king may get heat. So they sought for a fair damsel throughout all the coasts of Israel, and found Abishag a Shunammite, and brought her to the king. And the damsel was very fair, and cherished the king, and ministered to him: but the king knew her not…" (Vss 1-4). Let us pause here; you may read the rest of the story.

"King David grew old" is the way The Message translation puts it. And even though they pile blankets on him, he could not feel warmth or produce heat. What a pity! What are the points to note here? I mean, the president was old and could not produce heat even though a young woman of ravishing beauty was brought into him after a deliberate search all over the country, a project that must have gulped so much money from the nation's treasury. This is indeed a proven sign of a dead system.

The implications are quite obvious:

a. The presidency becomes tired and worn out
b. Thus, the executive arm of the government becomes overwhelmed, fatigued and exhausted
c. Logistics are halted for a while
d. Policies might be made but no execution or not speedily executed
e. Nonchalance may creep into other arms of government as a result
f. Leadership drive becomes passive and often redundant – zeal and enthusiasm hit the lowest ebb
g. No clear-cut direction and directives for the polity and economy
h. Economic and political activities may go on, but with everyone doing their thing, their own way (See Judges 21:25)
i. Executive councils may brainstorm and argue back and forth on possible ways to make a headway but all ideas may become counter-productive
j. Chances are that defections from the ruling party to the oppositions and vice versa may increase

The above points are just few of the possibilities or if you like, the probabilities and speculations that occur when a government or any other human organisms become very old or tired, dying or as good as dead. Have we not witnessed such scenes around us?

When tired or worn out organizations and dying or dead governments rule the nation's political or economic space, their deadness spreads into every other sector. It affects all and sundry. No matter what strategies they initiate and adopt to revive, resuscitate or resurrect such systems, nothing good comes of it. In the same way, when dead political parties emerge as the ruling party, no policies work out peace and progress no matter how many hot-heads they have as party chieftains.

Mr President was at the verge of death, but instead of his men to come to terms with the truth that it was time to infuse new blood and anoint a successor, they tried to revive the dead or fairer still, the dying man. And no matter how hard they tried, they failed and the virgin girl project became another white elephant project that put money in the pockets of few individuals who serve in the government.

But in the midst of these governments and organizations are people who should be separate. They are people being commanded to arise from the dead so that God can use them to found corporations that can truly change the narratives and transform the nation and her people. They are people who think they cannot stand on their own considering the enormous influence of the dead entities.

One thing I have observed over the years is that the stink and stench of dead people and dead organizations have really made it almost impossible to smell the aura of the living ones. As a result, the living ones tend to be drawn away to join the dead. I also observe that when men celebrated as legends who once had a name that they were alive but were truly dead, now die, they are better immortalized than those who truly lived out their God-designed purposes.

This quack and improper order of preference tempt the living legends to want to join the camp of the "dead". And in order to give the impression that they do not belong there, they create a scenario that they just want to get what they are looking for from the camp of the dead. But God has this to ask: **"Why seek ye the living among the dead?"** (Luke 24:5). That question by the Lord God is for the patriotic men to answer. It is a call to move from the dead; they have no living thing to offer!

SEEKING THE LIVING AMONG THE DEAD

One of the realities of life on earth is the existence of challenges or what most of us generally call problems. But we must take note that these challenges exist in our lives for reasons – either to build our resolve to stand up to them or break our resolve to rise above them. We determine the outcome by our response or reaction. Our responses or reactions to these challenges reveal who we really are, what we believe, and also to a large extent, where we reside our faith and rest our allegiance.

This last point is very crucial in determining the outcome of events in our mortal lives. The Holy Scripture says, **"Where a man's treasure is, will his heart be also"**. Wherever our minds wander to in times of challenges is undoubtedly where our faith lies. So, we must endeavour to set our mind on the right objects or subjects especially in time of challenges.

The most natural thing that happens when people face challenging times is to seek solutions. The first thing that fills our mind when we are facing problems or going through tough times is the thought of getting respite in the short run and in the long run.

Although a lot of people try to figure out immediate course of action to take to get solution, yet it is highly advisable to figure out the gains and regrets before grabbing any available solutions. This is because most available solutions are capable of throwing a people or a nation into retrogression and regrets. Solutions are meant to bring relief and comfort, and not otherwise. Therefore, we must be very careful of the solutions we seek and how we go about seeking them.

When Jesus Christ died and they buried Him, the women among His followers went to the tomb as usual to embalm His body. They were unaware that He had risen from the dead. When they could not find His body but rather saw angels in dazzling white robes, they were terrified. Then, the angels asked, ***"Why do you look for the living among [those who are] dead? He is not here, but has risen!"*** (Luke 24:4-6 AMP).

Before we go into reasons why people seek the living among the dead, let us see what seeking the living among the dead really means.

1. It means seeking solution where it cannot be found. It is natural for one to desire to have an end to their dilemma or dicey situations. But it is very important for them to seek the needed solution where it can be found.

Often we run into national challenges that price our national pride. Regrettably, the first thing our leaders or representatives do is to search on Google for help instead of praying to God first. They do not realize that the solution Google will give does not match the peculiarity of our problem in the country. Most of the answers on the internet are based on the experiences of nations and organizations with different challenges peculiar to them. They are not tailor-made to solve our problems.

Having said that, a people should know what exactly their problems are before brainstorming or running off in search of solutions. When the necessary analysis of the problems is not well carried out, any solution proffered will never bring respite, relief or expected result. This is why most of the solutions our country has sought from foreign lands never gave us the comfort we needed per time.

To seek help from countries we believe have the solution we believe that we need as a nation does not automatically mean such solutions when given to us will settle the matter. No! First things come first. Before we begin to look for help from certain places, we ought to carefully find out if such places have had our kind of experiences or challenges and overcome them. If no, then, seeking help from them would amount to seeking the living among the dead. This is because anything that cannot give life is dead itself. Hence, we must avoid running to people who have no life to give us as a nation.

2. It could also mean dealing with the symptoms while neglecting the root cause of the problem. This is very much the scenario here in my country. We find ourselves in a region and among a people who do not probe the past in order to deal with the present or prepare for the future. When we have a problem, we quickly think of a solution that comes cheap. Hence, we neglect the resourcefulness of research into what caused the problem in the first place so that we can address it once and for all. And for this neglect, we pay dearly with our lives and property.

I read a story in the Holy Bible – an account of a nation that suffered terribly because they were dealing with the symptoms instead of addressing the root of their national disaster. The account is found in the First Book of Samuel chapter five and chapter six.

After their war with the Israelites, the Philistines captured the Ark of God from Israel. That was a wrong catch and the beginning of their internal national tragedies. It started first with the judgement of their god, Dagon, and gradually moved into the city of Ashdod. From Ashdod, the tragedies spread to Gath, the birthplace of Goliath the giant.

But instead of the lords of the country – the senators, honourable representatives of the people, the military and other experts and major stakeholders of the country at all levels – to sit down and research, they continued with speculative measure in attempt to fix the national brouhaha.

Part of the account reads: **"God was hard on the citizens of Ashdod. He devastated them by hitting them with tumors. This happened in both the town and the surrounding neighbourhoods. He let loose rats among them. Jumping from ships there, rats swarmed all over the city! And everyone was deathly afraid. When the leaders of Ashdod saw what was going on, they decided, "The chest of the God of Israel has got to go. We can't handle this, and neither can our god Dagon." They called together all the Philistine leaders** (the clarion all) **and put it to them: "How can we get rid of the chest of the god of Israel?" the leaders agreed: "Move it to Gath." So they moved the Chest of the God of Israel to Gath."** (Vs. 6-8 TM) Emphasis mine

Now what really informed their conclusion to send the Ark of God to Gath? Bible history did not state their reason. But let me speculate with clues from Bible history:

- ❖ Gath was the birthplace of Goliath and his brothers – all giants who could stand any army
- ❖ Since these giants could stand the armies of Israel, they should be able to rise to the occasion – so they thought

- ❖ Gath was a stronghold of the Philistines where people take refuge and those after them never dared to go. For instance, when president-elect David Jesse ran away from home, he went and took refuge in Gath. And when the incumbent president of Israel, Saul Kish, heard of it, he never dared to go after David again (1 Samuel 27:4)

Nevertheless, the perceived permutations of the leaders of Ashdod that led to sending the Ark of God to Gath failed as history recorded that the trouble continued at Gath. Let me read further: **"But as soon as they moved it there, God came down hard on that city too. It was mass hysteria! He hit them with tumors. Tumors broke out on everyone in town, young and old. So they sent the Chest of God on to Ekron, but as the Chest was being brought into town, the people shouted in protest, "You'll kill us all by bringing in this Chest of the God of Israel!"**

Did you see that? Their presumed solution to the disaster was no solution at all! Yet, they kept speculating and experimenting, and thereby wasting lives and property.

When I look at the Nigerian and African episodes of tragedies, and the manners in which our leaders attempt to handle them or proffer solutions, I wonder if they are under some form of manipulation. Honestly,

I mean no insults. Some of them claim to be educated, intelligent, tested experts and technocrats, yet Nigeria and the African continent are bedevilled with horrifying and monstrous challenges that appear insurmountable and beyond remedy.

Sincerely speaking, and in my fair presumption, there is no problem that is facing any nation that cannot be solved or sorted out. The major problem lies with the so-called, self-acclaimed experts and technocrats who think they know it all. Their recommendations fall short of divine insight, which consequently results in constant experimentation with lives and property. Otherwise, our Nigerian leaders would not be switching from proposal of ranching to cattle colony and quite recently to RUGA – all in the bid to solve the farmers-herdsmen clashes. Yet, none ever worked.

Still, they continued to experiment at the expense of national unity and progress. None of them could think outside the box, but in the same unfruitful pattern capable of throwing the nation into retrogression, redundancy and regrets. Simply put: They were looking for the living among the dead!

Now, how did the leaders of the Philistines deliver their nation? And how can our leaders in Nigeria and the rest of Africa salvage our lands in a times like these? The answer is found in the following lines from our reliable Bible history:

"They called the Philistines leaders together and demanded, "Get it out of here, this Chest of the God of Israel. Send it back where it came from. We're threatened with mass death!" (I Samuel 5:11 TM)

That was the beginning of their deliverance – restitution! They came to a point where it dawned on them that they had been looking for solution from the wrong perspective all along. They realized that rotating the hosting of the stolen Ark of God – their wrong catch – from town to town was not yielding the desired solution.

In Nigeria, we must realize that the uncensored rotational presidency between the North and the South might not be the joker to determine our winning the war against nepotism, tribal disharmony, social inequality and other forms of headache we have been having since independence in 1960.

Our leaders must come to the realization that speculative prescriptions to our national maladies and misappropriations cannot produce economic boom or political stability. And whatever we do, we have to hurry to get us out of the dead so that we do not end up dead!

The Ekronites had to protest the decision of the Philistine lords to transport the Ark of God of Israel, their looted treasury, into their territory. Folks, protest did not start today. It did not start in this contemporary age. It has been before we arrived this era of democracy and even before the colonization and military dispensations that came before. The protest was heavy. The Ekronites did not hold back their angst; they let it out in serious protest: ***"You'll kill us all by bringing in this Chest of the God of Israel!"***

The Ark of God was a blessing to Israel and her people but had become a curse to the Philistines and their country. One man's meal is another's poison. The American dream works well for the Americans. The Chinese dream may work well for those people in the largest and most populous country of the world. The Britons have what blesses them in their land but such can bruise us here in Nigeria.

Our leaders across board especially the national leaders should sit down and find what will work for us in this most populous country in Africa! The importation of American, British or Chinese ideologies and policies that are anti-Nigeria should stop. We are tired of seeking solution from dead ends that apparently become dead on arrival. Nigeria is a blessed land, not a burial ground! What then must we do? We must take a cue from the Philistines.

The leaders of the Philistines tried another strategy they had probably neglected for long. It was the heavy protest by the people of Ekron that pushed them to consider this last option, which turned out the best option ever. Our most reliable Bible history record says, **"After the Chest of God had been among the Philistine people for seven months, the Philistine leaders called together their religious professionals, the priests, and experts on the supernatural for consultation: "How can we get rid of this Chest of God, get it of our hands without making things worse? Tell us!"** (6:1-2 TM). This is it!

Can our people begin to ask from the right quarters? Can our leaders in Nigeria begin to seek solution from those Heaven has planted in their midst to guide them in the way to national prosperity? All through history especially as recorded by the Holy Bible, which is the most authentic history record, nations and kingdoms only survived through the wise and unfailing counsel of prophets and priests who God used at sundry times.

The nation of Israel, for instance, is surrounded by hostile nations but they have always survived by the ministry of men and women who God sent to them from the earliest times. The surrounding nations treated the God of Israel and His prophets with a jaunty wave of the hand, and suffered terrible defeats in the hands of their enemies and oppressors. Even when the children of Israel did the same, they also suffered setbacks and serious blows from enemy countries.

We must not allow such negative history accounts repeat in our collective existence as a nation under God. The Philistines suffered severely from Ashdod to Gath to Ekron and all over their country because they neglected the source of permanent solution – God. Simply put: They sought the living among the dead. Notwithstanding, they found a way out. How? By engaging those divinely empowered to proffer permanent solution.

"…the Philistine leaders called together their religious professionals, the priests, and experts on the supernatural for consultation…They said, "If you're going to send the Chest of the God of Israel back, don't just dump it on them. Pay compensation. Then you will be healed. After you're in the clear again, God will let up on you. Why wouldn't he?" (1 Samuel 6:1-3 TM).

What is my point here? It is to point us all to the only source of solution there is for every kind of trouble in a nation. We must learn from our National Anthem to call on "the God of Creation to direct our noble cause".

How do we get to see God, then? Unfortunately, He does not have His High Commission at Abuja. He has no liaison office at Johannesburg. But He has men and women who He has appointed as His commissioners, ambassadors and regents all over the country.

They are wise people who only the wise will seek to consult on national, regional, constituency or community matters. The Philistine leaders consulted their priests and religious professionals. Our leaders should learn to do so back here in the country.

Although we have some men of God so called, who have tainted the ecclesiastical institution with the mud of unholy life-style, yet there are men and women in both the ecclesiastical and non-ecclesiastical sectors who are clean. These professionals have polished pedigree and impeccable integrity, and are ready to offer their loyal service to the nation. Their target is to contribute to the pursuit of peace and prosperity of this great nation – no more!

Hence, the helmsmen at Aso Rock and Apo Quarters should not waste further time and national resources in seeking help that rarely comes from the abroad. They should rather channel all they have within their constitutional ambient to seek these array of men out from every nook and cranny of the country without any form of prejudice.

Consultation with these special breed of people has become imminent to finding lasting solutions to the myriads of maladies besieging this beautiful land. If the "uncircumcised" philistines found their priests and experts in the supernatural useful and their counsel worked, our leaders across board should bury their pride and reach out to men who God can use for us. It is time to stop looking elsewhere – the living among the dead!

REASONS AND RESULTS OF SEEKING THE LIVING AMONG THE DEAD

I have actually written more on the last point of seeking solutions from dead ends than I intended to. Honestly, I could not stop the flow of thoughts and inspiration. I think it is worth the time, anyways. Now, I want us to look at the question in Luke 24:4, **"Why do you look for the living among the dead?"**

If we go back to the portion in the Holy Bible, we will see there was no reply to that question. This means those women led by Mary of Magdala could not answer the question. Clearly, the angels that asked the question did not waste time in directing them to where their quest would be solved – Galilee! So they rushed off excitingly to where solution was waiting.

But, right here, I will try to give some highlights why people seek the living from the dead. I mean the reasons why they seek solution where it cannot be found. It is the same thing as dealing with the symptoms instead of the root.

1. **They do not know the way**. When people do not know the way, they follow any direction as long as it leads them to somewhere. They become blind followers of the blind. The disciples of Jesus Christ believed that He was still lying in the tomb at the cemetery. So they went there.

Our leaders still expect that solutions to our national challenges are with the British or Europeans so they go there each time they run into a storm. The fact that our colonial masters are among the world super powers does not mean they have the solutions to our issues. What we do not seem to understand is that God is the Real Master over Nigeria and every other nation.

Even the United States of America that was colonized by the Great Britain does not run each time to them for help the way our leaders in Nigeria do. The US enshrined a strong attestation of their dependence on God on their national currency: IN GOD WE TRUST. This shows that they know the way to follow to get the solution they need as a country.

Jesus Christ declared that He is the Way, the Truth and the Life. This means that it is only when our nation embraces this Truth would they be able to know the way. There is a way that seems right to a nation, but the end of it is destruction – a dead end.

2. They seek solution from the wrong places because **they do not know their God**. The Word of God Almighty says, ***"They that know their God shall be strong, and shall do exploits"*** (Daniel 11:32). This verse of the inspired Word of God is very instructive because it talks about knowing – knowledge and the application of it is power.

The solution every nation seeks is knowledge-based. Whether solution to economic or political instability, it has to do with level of knowledge. The disciples of Jesus Christ went in search of Him at the cemetery because they did not know that He was risen from the dead. If they knew, they would not have rushed to the cemetery very early morning to seek him out. Rather, they would have gone to Galilee to meet their Master there.

President Solomon David admonished in his book of proverbs, ***"Get knowledge…"*** (Proverbs 4:7). Further in chapter twenty four, he makes a strong case for knowledge and understanding. Knowledge comes from careful study and understanding comes from God. Without knowledge there shall be no understanding. This is because we cannot understand what we do not know or seek to know. Knowledge is key to solving problems. And the knowledge of God who gives understanding comes top.

Challenges will always overwhelm any nation if they or their leaders do not know God. I am not talking about being religious, but about knowing God. Why is it so?

a. **They cannot be strong.** That is, they will not be able to summon the needed courage or develop the unwavering resolve to tackle the challenges. President Saul Kish was an example of a leader who could not keep appointment with God and so his kingly rule fell to pieces. What was responsible for his betrayal of divine appointment? Simply put: He did not fully know the God that called him into office and how He worked with His servants.

The marginal knowledge of God could not help him from becoming fearful at the sight of the opposition and so he crumbled before them. He knew people of power – his political friends and generals in his army – that he feared them more than God. And at the nick of time when he faced a serious challenge to his government, he failed to identify the only Source of strength and salvation – GOD!

b. **They cannot do exploits.** The truth is that no man can accomplish anything worthy of praise without a god. So also, no one can attract exploits that receive divine endorsement without divine insight from God! Without understanding God and how He works, great exploits will remain a delusion. We must all come to the realization that only those who know the God of Heaven that can really accomplish great things.

3. Most people seek solution from the wrong places because of **wrong affiliations**. When a nation is affiliated with the wrong people or countries, they are compelled to seek solution or help from them. The Holy Word of God says, ***"Evil communications corrupt good manners"*** (1 Corinthians 15:33). That is, evil associations corrupt good people!

Bible history recorded about a certain president of Judah of ancient time whose name was Asa, a descendant of the wisest president that ever lived – Solomon David. He was a good man who did things right in God's sight. God delivered him and his country several times from challenges that would have wiped the nation out.

However, in the thirty-six year of his reign as president and commander in chief of Judah, he went into affiliation with the president of Syria (Aram), Ben-Hadad, whom God considered an infidel and idolatrous man. The nation of Syria at that time stunk before God. So He became very furious with President Asa.

History records: ***"Just after that, Hanani the Seer came to Asa King of Judah and said, "Because you went for help (became ally with) to the king of Aram and didn't ask God for help, you've lost a victory over the army of*** *king of Aram. Didn't the Ethiopians and Libyans come against you with superior forces, completely outclassing you with chariots and cavalry? But you asked God for help and he gave you the victory; God is always on the alert, constantly on the lookout for people who are totally committed to him. You were foolish to go for human help when you could have God's help. Now you're in trouble – one round of war after another"* (2 Chronicles 16:7-9 TM).

We can see from the above stated piece of authentic biblical history what lack of wisdom which leads to wrong affiliation can do to a leader and his nation. In the book, Vanity Republic **– the Errors of our Heroes Past, Volume 5** – the author stressed that the foolishness of leaders usually attract divine sentence against their people. It was the foolish act of David Jesse in 2 Samuel chapters 11 and 24 that brought judgement on his immediate family and the nation of Israel respectively. It was the defection of President Solomon David in 1 Kings 11 that attracted judgment on his descendants and by extension, to Israel his country.

When the leaders of any nation go into any form of affiliations with the wrong people or countries, they attract the curse on such nations and their people as well. Hence the clarion call is to all our leaders to begin to withdraw their allegiance from such nations and people who have contributed to our national woes.

Collectively as a nation, we must redefine our affiliations and associations. This is because associations influence decisions in times of challenges. In challenging times, people usually run to their allies who are in the position to support them.

There is nothing wrong with seeking help. Howbeit, if our allies are the wrong ones, we will end up seeking help from a dead end. John Mason said, *"Never receive counsel from unproductive people...Never discuss your problems with someone incapable of contributing to the solution because those who never succeeded themselves are always the first to tell you how."* That was what happened to President Asa of Judah. We must not allow such negative piece of history repeat in our contemporary existence.

Now, remember that I said earlier that seeking the living among the dead is like dealing with symptoms instead of the root cause. Why do people do this?

a. The root cause is not easily detected like the symptoms. A rot could stay for decades in a system before its symptoms begin to show up. These symptoms usually show up when the damage has been done. In this case, it is often the negligence of the early warning signs that something is wrong within a system. Today, our country is showing many signs and symptoms of a failing society, but these did not sprout out today. They have been there pointing to the fact that something is not right all along, but the people neglected it.

Take, for example, the heightened level of insecurity in the country. The onslaught by Boko Haram, the different shades of kidnapping and ritual killing, the threat by the influx of uncensored strangers from across the sub-Saharan countries, and the killer herders popularly tagged Fulani herdsmen. All these symptoms did not show up at once in these current times.

There have been calls from various quarters on those saddled with the task of responding to these issues to rise to the challenge, but they treated the calls as false alarm. The custodians became so lazy to investigate or verify those calls, hence, allowing time for the situations to escalate into full-fledged nuisance to the society. We ought to take responsibility for our actions and inactions.

b. It takes much less cost to deal with symptoms than with the root cause. It takes thorough diagnosis to really discover and deal with the source of a chronic issue. This thorough or deep diagnosis costs so much. Though the cost varies from the nature to the scope, yet it takes due diligence to tackle it. For example, headache could be a symptom of a bigger health issue, but it takes only a pain reliever such as paracetamol to calm it. Meanwhile, to discover the real source or what triggers the headache would take careful and close examination by a health practitioner. There may be need to carry out some medical tests to ascertain what next to do.

The truth is that these tests cost more, no doubt, but carrying them out is the right thing to do – the right way to go! When a people fail to address the root cause of regional restiveness, ethnic escalations, and societal skirmishes in the country, their first response when the situation has become irredeemable is to seek quick remedies. We ought to be a people who deal with issues of common interest holistically and within redeemable timelines.

CHAPTER THREE
THE CLARION CALL

"There's a call comes ringing o'er the restless waves
Send the light… send the light!
There are souls to rescue, there are souls to save
Send the light… send the light

Send the light, the blessed gospel light
Let it shine from shore to shore
Send the light, the blessed gospel light
Let it shine forever more.

This ancient hymn reminds me of the word that Apostle Paul got in a night vision, **"Come over to Macedonia and help us!"** (Acts of the Apostles 16:9). He and his team responded immediately by sailing all the way into that part of Europe. Today. The call is as relevant as it was in Paul's days. This time, the Macedonians are not the ones calling, Nigerians and all Africans are the people in need and are placing the call.

The call is to all Nigerians and Africans both at home and in the Diaspora to come to the help of the country. This is a country with the largest economy in Africa yet described as the headquarters of poverty in the Cush continent. This call is to salvage what is left from the plundering of the collective revenue from crude oil explorations in the 7th largest producer of crude in the whole world, yet with no single functioning refinery as it stands.

In this chapter, we shall look at the necessity of the call and the need to heed the call. It has become highly imperative for all and sundry to be reminded of the significance of our National Anthem. If we must build a nation where peace and justice shall reign, and where equity ad fairness prevail, then, now is the time to be serious with responding to this call.

THE NECESSITY OF THE CALL

In 2010 when the late President Umaru Musa Yar'adua was deathly sick, rumours of his demise filtered into the Nigeria's political space from a UK medical facility, causing some tension in the country. The "kitchen cabinet", as it was reported in the news, of the Yar'adua presidency was alleged to have dismissed the rumours of his death as fallacious and unfounded with the intention of holding on to the reins of power or buying time to tighten some loose ends in case the game changed.

Naturally and constitutionally too, his then vice president, Dr Goodluck Jonathan who was holding brief as acting president and commander in chief was expected to take over as the Number One citizen of the country. There were several calls from major players in the polity and economy on the constituted authorities to do the needful – to come out clean with the truth of Mr President's health status. The callers demanded that if he was dead, power should be handed over to the lucky Goodluck Jonathan. It was such a crucial time in the general history of the giant of Africa.

I remember vividly how the National Assembly rowed over the matter and eventually the Nigeria's Senate under Mr David Mark came up with the "Doctrine of Necessity". Whatever was the merit for such submission, one thing was certain: that coinage somehow nipped in the bud further agitations that could have led to serious aggravations that we now witness in recent times. Simply put: that move by the Upper Chamber saved the day and became almost a norm in our everyday collective existence. Hence I feel pressed also to import that doctrine in this renewed call to my countrymen for a better reason.

If the doctrine of necessity succeeded in saving us a major setback in our political journey in the time of our "nascent" democracy, how much more now in this time that Nigerians are struggling not for political stability but for the survival of the nation and her people.

If a David mark's inspired doctrine of necessity attracted a general nod of accentuation at that time, this present call should be given an unbiased and unanimous vote of acceptance by all and sundry – elites and commons inclusive.

If in the dispensation of relative peace and economic stability, that call was considered a doctrine, then in this time of pain and unprecedented youth restiveness, we must consider the call a strong dogma.

This is not a time to plague it with religious prejudice or ethnic sentiment because these are factors that have hampered several calls for national unity, peace and advancement. At all costs, we must avoid towing these lines that our greedy and insensitive politicians have designed as templates for the country. We have just one choice to make: To treat this renewed call as very crucial to our collective survival, success and sustenance as a great nation and good people.

Now, why is this call so crucial? Why must we treat it as a veritable avenue for our success? The following points or reasons are only a few.

1. Patriotism

We need compatriots. The call to arise is to compatriots. If any nation must survive and succeed, it is the responsibility of its citizens who by birth or otherwise became so. The citizens, however, cannot make their country successful unless they are patriotic in every sense of the word.

This patriotism is not a feeling of being a part of the country or mere pledging of loyalty to it. It is such that drives them to actively participate in its affairs through private or public partnership. It is not enough to carry about national identification but to be real stakeholders who share in the nation's assets and liabilities, conquests and challenges, and stand with her through thick and thin moments.

True patriotism is pivoted on love and loyalty, strong belief in and sound behaviour toward all its components or compositions. If we decide to go down memory lane, we would be able to find only few dozens of citizens who were truly patriotic to this country.

Sadly too, most of the people who have been decorated with national honours and celebrated as national icons are far from the real definition of patriotic citizens. We do not take our definition of patriotism from politicians or bureaucrats; their standard fall below the accepted standard on the global stage.

Although we cannot deny the facts that some of them have performed credibly well in their service to the nation, yet we cannot fully ascribe the noble status of patriotic citizenship to them. This is because their kind of patriotism is predicated upon self-love and partisan loyalty, which contrast the true meaning of patriotism.

The Wiktionary defines patriotism as *"love of country and devotion to the welfare of one's compatriots"*. It is also the virtues and actions of someone who truly loves and zealously supports and defends their country. People who are patriotic have a rare passion that inspires them to serve their country. They are not motivated by the privileges of the offices they aspire to sit and serve. Rather, they are driven by the desire to entrench enduring values in the system and by deep affection for the people of their constituency or country.

Let me bullet these points for better understanding.

A. **Love of the Country**.

   Love is a universal language. It is a language that actions convey better than words. A language that breaks barriers, crosses coasts of countries, calms any chaotic situation, and quenches the embers of hate. Yet, it is the language that has suffered so much abuse by those who profess it but hardly practise it.

Love conquers all – not to subjugate them but to salvage and serve. God's Word in the Holy Bible says, **"For God so loved the world that he gave his only begotten son, that whosoever believeth in him should not perish, but have everlasting life"** (John 3:16).

God is not selfish. He showers His love on all – every country under the sun is included in His love. Both the good and the bad, partisan and non-partisan, bond or free, elites or commons – come under the canopy of His love. As people made in His image, it behoves us to follow His good example. Since God loves all the countries of the earth, are we not supposed to love our country?

Love of the country is beyond words that entice the citizens. It begins with the realization of the fact of God's love for the people of the country. Words are not enough, actions that are geared toward building and improving the lives of the people should do the talking.

Bible history records that **"David now realized why the Lord made him king** (president, senator, chief executive officer, traditional ruler, governor) **and blessed his kingdom** (presidency, administration) **so greatly – it was because God wanted to pour out his kindness on Israel, his chosen people"** (2 Samuel 5:12 TLB, Emphasis mine).

When God gives a people their leaders, He does so for the love of the country. The leaders must realize this. You have no mandate from the people, but from God! He is the Creator of the leadership institution and Designer of the saddle you sit on. The people only confirm your choice through electioneering process.

Read these lines from the scripture book we cited above: ***"Representatives of all the tribes of Israel now came to David at Hebron and gave him their pledge of loyalty. "We are your blood brothers…the Lord has said that you should be the shepherd and leader of his people"…and they crowned him king of Israel"*** (vs.1-4 TLB).

It was God who first chose David Jesse as president and commander in chief of his country, Israel. The people knew this and came together to confirm his presidency. Any politician or leader of a nation must know this. As time went by, David Jesse realized that it was because of God's love for his country that He made him president. God wanted to pour out His kindness and tender love on Israel, hence He chose a vessel in the person of David Jesse.

Dear leader, you are not on that saddle by your political orchestrations. You are there by divine ordination so that you can be a channel of God's kindness to your country. So you cannot afford to show hatred for any section or region of your country. You must not be biased in your conduct toward your country. The love of the leader for his country is the attestation of this realization.

Any leader who is prejudiced in his love for his country only denies God as the One who installed him as the leader. It will also be a clear betrayal of his divine appointment or election if he shows nepotism, showers favouritism and stands against the right of a region in his country.

So, you are expected by this call to begin to show love for all the regions, ethnic groups, tribes and everyone in your country. David Jesse realized this and God blessed his kingdom greatly. Follow his example and let God bless your administration with peace and prosperity.

B. **Devotion to Citizens' Welfare**

Devotion follows love. This is to say that there will be no devotion without love. That is why we discussed love as the first ingredient of patriotism. This next one is very vital too. Devotion means to wholly and completely give one's attention or focus to the all-round well-being of the citizens. All forms of calling are for service to humanity. Whether it is political, religious or traditional in nature, they are designed to bless the people of the country or the continent.

It is not enough for politicians or other saddle-seekers to rollout their manifestos – promising to serve the people. It is not sufficient to advertise your "good" intentions for the people whose support you seek on television, radio and billboards across the country or state. You must be prepared for the real task after your elections.

I have observed with utmost dismay – and this is common knowledge – how the same people who devote so much time and money to political campaigns begin to tell stories for the gods when they assume leadership. This is irresponsibility! You claim to have love for your country but you turn away from the needs of the people of the country. I mean, something is wrong with such leaders!

If we look at David Jesse's story again in 2 Samuel 8:15, history tells us, **"David reigned with justice over Israel and was fair to everyone"** (TLB). Did you see that? Being fair to everyone, not to some people. This act can only come from a heart so devoted to the people. Devotion breeds fairness – good consideration of all who come under your leadership influence.

This devotion of David Jesse did not end with him as commander in chief, it continued after he was long off the scene. His successor, Solomon David, did even more in this regard. Bible history did not leave us without reference to his outstanding acts of devotion to the welfare of his people. He outperformed all leaders of his time in this matter. If we look at his example as recorded in the Holy Scriptures, we see how devotion to the people's well-being can promote a nation.

After his inauguration as president and commander in chief of his country, President Solomon David paid tribute to God first at Gibeon, showing off his devotion to Him in a grand style. His Excellency sacrificed a thousand whole burnt offerings to God on a single night. And that singular but weighty move attracted the Almighty God to him that same night, asking what he wanted from Him.

In another display of devotion for his countrymen he replied, ***"Give me an understanding mind so that I can govern your people well and know the difference between what is right and what is wrong. For who by himself is able to carry such a heavy responsibility?"*** (1 Kings 3:9 TLB). This request by His Excellency was borne out a heart ready to devotedly serve the people of his country.

To really know leaders who are committed to the welfare of the people, check out their requests before higher authorities. A local council chairman who has the interest of his local government at heart will put their needs before his own needs. A governor who is devotedly given to his people will never be found sponsoring violence or inciting ethnic rivalries in the state, but will campaign for peace.

To know how devoted a leader is, the lifestyle or standard of living of the common people tells the story. It is not what we see on the pages of newspapers while the people continue to live in penury and penniless year after year. President Solomon David gave serious attention to his countrymen to the point that ***"all their needs were met; they ate and drank and were happy"*** (vs.20 TM).

God's record about this cannot be false because it further states that ***"throughout the lifetime of Solomon, all of Judah and Israel lived in peace and safety; and each family had its own home and garden."*** (Vs 25 TLB). Only God and those people could tell how it looked back in those days.

Devotion to the welfare of the citizens should form the premise for legislative discourses in our legislative assemblies at states and federal levels. Over the years our lawmakers have not done well in this area. It took years to even finalize on the Petroleum Industrial Bill and yet as at this time, debates are still on to decide the true fate of the citizens and communities affected by the necessary evil of oil exploration.

Devotion to the citizens will make any sitting governor, legislator, president, etc., to rise to put an end to the rampaging banditry and kidnapping that have become a lifestyle for trouble makers especially in the Northern regions of the country. Insecurity is mounting because the security architecture is yet to become serious with taming the tide. With the foregoing, those leaders are yet to imbibe the spirit of devotion.

We cannot really exhaust the discourse on devotion and its significance to nation building. There is a slogan in the country that says "Good People, Great Nation". This means that it is good people that make good nation. Conversely, bad people make a bad nation. Furthermore, it takes a people who have been made good to equally make the nation good.

Can we then say that the problem of our dear nation is with the quality of people her leaders have been producing? And when I say leaders, I mean everyone in the position of influence from the smallest family to the biggest corporate entity.

In the same way, the same poor quality citizenry produces poor quality leadership, and vice versa. So you see the cycle: bad leadership – bad people – bad leaders! This is the cycle we must break. One of the ways to break this cycle is by giving adequate attention to producing good people through strong social welfare policies and packages.

C. **Defence of the Territory from Invasion.** This is the last ingredient of this discourse on being a patriotic citizen. Remember we are looking at the necessity for this call to stand with the country. And it is important we look at this point too – defending the country against invasion by both external and internal forces.

I would not want to dwell so much on this because much of it has been said in previous chapters. "To defend her unity…" as we see in our National Pledge is a serious call. The unity of a country is the bedrock for sustainable prosperity. No nation prospers in disunity and division. Hence, the citizens including the leaders should not compromise whatever it would take to maintain a united country.

Defence of the country includes but not limited to protecting the indigenous peoples from exploitation by foreigners; protecting their languages from adulteration; guarding the moral code of the nation from abuse; ensuring the economy of the nation is not hijacked by foreign interests, etc. Apart from guarding the territorial boundaries of the country, the real work of defence is mostly internal. This is because a country can easily disintegrate from within as the case of many nations of the world.

In a time like the one we are in, we are in serious need of patriots who will do anything to defend the country especially in the areas I mentioned above. The agitation by the various indigenous peoples in the country is a result of neglect by those destiny saddled with the duty of defence. No one wants to live in a land where they are neglected and abandoned to fate especially at the backdrop of great abundance of resources. Such scenario breeds angst and agitation for division.

Language is what makes a people unique. In Nigeria, we are blessed to have many tribes with their unique tongues. Unfortunately, our first nationalists did not see the need for these tribes to maintain their tongues as seen in other climes with diverse ethnicity. Rather, their quest for independence blinded them to that reality that we can maintain our unique tongues in a united nation.

While adopting the language of the colonizers was important for the coordination of the country at the time, destroying our original and natural languages in the attempt is most regrettable. Countries such as China, India, Korea, and others in Asia speak their different tongues even though they were colonized by the same people that colonized us. So, why is our case different? It is because those who should defend this very important part of us failed to see the need.

Some researchers have found and published it that so many languages would be extinct by the year 2050. And going by the trend in Nigeria, some of our mother tongues would be among them. Today, we find it difficult to even speak our mother tongues in community confines. The Lingual Franca has taken over control of our tongues. And the most worrisome aspect of it is that the leadership of the peoples across board see no necessity to do something about it. This is why this call has become highly necessary.

Morality is the heart of character. The way of life of a people swings around it. When I was a little boy, I saw how our people lived a communal life. Everyone especially an elder is a stakeholder. No single parent was the sole custodian of his children. It was a time when a disobedient child or misbehaving adult was the responsibility of everyone who could make impact on them for a change. People came together more peacefully to do common work to benefit all. It was like the early apostolic dispensation where no one actually laid claims to any material thing; everyone owned everything – the same thing. Today, it is a different but painful scenario.

To close this discourse on the defence of the country from invasion, we must look at the economy. The reality staring us in the face is the daylight hijack going on in the country and the continent. Foreigners have taken up almost every productive and lucrative sector of our economic life.

Oil and gas, which is the main stay of the country is already in the hands of foreign investors. Manufacturing of essential commodities that used to be our pride as a nation fell into decay while foreign merchants took over. And the worst is that they do the manufacturing in their countries and ship in the finished products into our land, making us largely consumers.

It is good to have foreign investors in the country but whereby they become the masters while the indigenous people take the back row is worrisome. Capital flight becomes the result and deficient human capital development leaves our people out of future strides in the economic sector.

When we put these in proper perspective, the chief custodians of our economy will do all in their constitutional powers to correct the imbalance. We must see to it that our people own and drive the economy as it stands in other developed countries such as China, Singapore, South Korea and India.

CHAPTER FOUR
HEED THE CALL

"But be ye doers of the word, and not hearers only, deceiving your own selves." – James 1:22

"(For not the hearers of the law are just before God, but the doers of the law shall be justified" – Romans 2:13.

When it comes to doing the thing, most people are quite guilty. What we do at best is talk and make laws that are hardly followed by the people. Even the lawmakers are not free in this regard of keeping the laws they make. A very big issue about walking the talk keeps slowing down our progress as a nation and a continent. We must not continue to be such a people.

As a people who desire and yearn for national prosperity, we must be proactive and action-driven at all times. The customary behaviour of procrastinating and postponing issues of national interests must give way to a tradition of doing the needful, and that on time. Doing the needful entails taking a look at what has been proposed to provide solutions, what we have done so far, and what we should do to ensure that we accomplish our national dreams, if truly we have them well-defined.

The Nigerian and African states have gone through hellish experiences that have left the people unsure of their future. All over the Cush continent and her countries, many are still going through so much turmoil in almost all critical sectors. The urgent need to save the future of the continent has been a major concern for well-meaning stakeholders. But the actions taken so far have only served as palliative measures rather than solve the problems at the core.

Some people especially groups all over the continent have taken the responsibility to address the abnormalities that have been so far highlighted in this call. However, the impact recorded so far has been slim compared to the expectations of both the initiators and the beneficiaries. The real deal rests on the shoulders of the people saddled with the greater responsibility of providing the roadmap for the rest to follow. And until these roadmaps are clearly communicated to the grassroots, we may continue in this quandary for a little longer time.

It is particularly worrisome that these prime custodians are only fast-tracking issues that bother on select individual interests rather than on the general or public interests. It has been one forum or expo yet the core issues that tend to divide us further apart are not vigorously pursued to an acceptable conclusion. Issues of security of lives and property, inter-tribal disharmonies, human trafficking across the sub-

Saharan cities, and internal leadership or political eruptions, which have been on the front burners, seem to get slow resolutions. And it has been the expectations of the average citizens to see a more robust approach in attacking these matters headlong thus putting us back on top as the giant of Africa.

If we take the issue of security for instance, we will find that the nation has not really heeded the call of compatriots as enshrined in our National Anthem. What has been happening across the countries of Africa in recent times leaves much to be desired of our leadership. Most especially in the second decade into this 21st Century, we can clearly see body language revealing negligence, unpreparedness, lack of innovativeness, and massive incompetence among the major executives in the sector.

When the news of invasion of non-nationals hit the national news space, little did the leadership understand the degree of menace it would cause if left inadequately addressed. Instead of focussing on that core issue, the blame game between political gladiators took over the news screens.

A look at 2014-2015, the insurgents increased their fierce attacks from the North-East part of the country. Some of them rebranded as herdsmen busy infiltrating the North-Central region coupled with kidnapping in the south. If not for some sensitive well-meaning citizens in the public sector who were screaming out their dissatisfaction with the response by leadership, we would not even know where this beautiful country would have been by now.

The leadership failed to understand that terrorists and all who make a living putting nations into discomforting situations target election and leadership transition years, the death of national leaders or icons, and even major shake-ups in the security architecture of a country.

So when politicians are busy plotting how to undo one another in electioneering campaigns, these brutes also get busy plotting how to overthrow the country or some key sections of it. And because our type of democracy does not provide a robust framework for the participation of the ordinary people, our people decide in favour of apathy and hopelessness.

Although this hopeless and apathetic disposition of the people of the country is not helping in any way, it is the result of deliberate exclusion of the people at the grassroots in decision and policy making in the country. It is only during the months preceding general elections that our democratic proponents realize the usefulness of the people. It is when they need the votes of the people that they realize their voices count in the business of the country. This is not supposed to be so in this era where every right-thinking nation on the earth seeks to rise from the ashes of backwardness to join the comity of prosperous nations.

So in this wise, I am calling on all our people at various strata to rise to emancipate our dear land from the clutches of all kinds of vices and vulgar elements. To enable all heed this call to the defence of fatherland, we must reiterate our commitments to serve our land with love and strength and faith as the Anthem beckons. Since I have talked about love for the country in the last chapter before this, we will do well to have faith.

Most of us especially those outside the confraternity of the elite and political class are worse hit by loss of faith in our country. The mismanagement and misappropriation of our collective resources by the elite and political class are responsible for this lack of faith. We have allowed their vagaries to birth our vagrancy and variance in our belief system. The faith of our fathers which we once held sacred has become a tale on the lips of most of us. This sad development is the reason potential stakeholders have taken to seeking greener pastures abroad rather than invest their ingenuity into the Nigerian project.

Faith in the fatherland is a strong determinant in achieving a prosperous nation. When people that should believe begin to doubt the prospects and potentials that abound in their country, a lot of bad things begin to happen as unintended consequences.

At the level I am writing from, this is the worst deficiency quotient menacing our existence as a nation.

When people lose faith, they import paralysis and polarization into the core of our beings. This situation pushes the people into either of the extremes – exploiting the system through legitimate loopholes or experimenting with criminalities in an I-do-not-care manner. This has never helped any nation that truly wants to be a giant in every area. This is a serious challenge that must be holistically addressed through the various channels the governments have created to do so.

To be able to get the citizens believe in the Nigerian project, and by extension, the African project, there must be a concerted effort by all the agencies saddled with such responsibilities and coordinated by the Ministry of Information and Culture. The National Orientation Agency domiciled in all the states are expected to embark on mass enlightenment campaigns targeting the key stakeholders as well as the emerging shareholders in the national project. To be fair to all, these agencies did not do much in the early 21st Century to engraft the emerging stakeholders who are the controllers of the economy and polity two decades after.

I feel the major challenge at the beginning of the 21st century was the military hangover around the new democratic Nigerian state. Our democratic progenitors were yet to grasp the realities and restraints that come with embracing a democracy. So they somehow continued with most of the ideas and inventions of their military predecessors that never worked in the favour of our prosperity. These actions in no small measure contributed in throwing the citizens into deeper doubts about the integrity of the leadership. And the disbelief about the workability of the Nigerian project grew worse.

But after about two decades of experimenting with this new way of life, our governments should do the needful. To be fair again, the ministries and agencies have been trying to build faith in the people once again. There have been slogans such as Good People, Great Nation and Change Begins with Me. There have also been similar campaigns by states to instil the right spirit of faith in the heart of the people. To an extent, these campaigns have worked but the people's heart have been wounded that it will take more than campaigns to heal.

In the next chapter, which is usually my traditional way of concluding all my books, I will share my strong submissions on how we can get into the hearts of the different people of the country for our collective blessings. It will be sheer waste of our scarce national resources to continue to embark on campaigns without considering the people we claim to target with such campaigns.

CHAPTER FIVE

RANDOM PERSPECTIVES

I feel so relieved of a heavy burden that have been on my heart for a long time. It usually does not take me so much time to complete writing a book like this, but this one is a special one. It is not special in the sense that I was inspired to write it from the Nigeria's National Anthem and Pledge, which are sacred oaths of our founding fathers. It is special because of its significance to the time we now live in.

Just like The Errors of our Heroes Past, volumes one to five that God inspired and instructed me to write in 2011, which also has its import from the National Anthem, this book has so much content that wraps up the essence of being a sovereign state. If you have read the Errors of our Heroes Past series, which include Lean Freedom Fat Slavery (Vol.1); Leadership without Successorship (Vol.2); Partisan Politics (Vol.3); Executive Lawlessness (Vol.4) and Vanity Republic (Vol.5), then you will agree that God is so much interested in our affairs.

But if you have not read them, you may kindly visit amazon.com to get the full copies of each book. Whereas that series featured the lives and times of some key national leaders in Bible times, this book differs as it presents the realities of our present existence as you must have noticed while reading it. It was deliberate so as to capture the essence and communicate the message to all concerned – including you and me.

Humanity is besieged by so many challenges. One of the problems I see that is worst with us is the attitude of taking things for granted. It makes us less the image of God that we were created to be. Truth is there is nothing much different between us and the animals in the forest or waters. We breathe, they do. We feed, they do the same. We breed and they do also. In fact, we have some difficulties breeding normally, but hardly do we see these animals suffer barrenness or still birth.

We can hardly see a goat go through a caesarean session to have her kid, but our women suffer that a lot. How the ants and reptiles multiply remains a mystery to millions of people, yet we claim superiority over them. And indeed we are superior and special. But what makes us special is not any of these abilities, which lower animals easily possess. What makes us special is the nature of our Creator that should reflect in our dealings with one another and the environment. Unfortunately, we have come behind in this area.

We were created to reflect God Almighty who made us in His image and after His likeness. "Like God, he made us" is what we read in His Holy Book – the Bible. We are not expected to be different from Him. His nature is that of love, justice, fairness, faithfulness and holiness. These are attributes that should distinguish us from other created beings. Our ability to relate with ourselves and our environment in the same ways that God deals with us will show that we are truly special.

God so loves us that He is patient with us. He understands our limitations and challenges, and has generously made provisions for us to overcome our weaknesses. He expects us to take advantage of these provisions to live a fulfilled life according to His will for us on earth. These provisions guarantee peace, prosperity and passionate affection for our fellow countrymen. But it is our responsibility to accept them and use them to make life beautiful here on earth.

A beautiful life on this planet earth is possible. The forests, oceans and deserts are meant to serve us. The wind and the sea waves should bring us a breath of fresh air. God made it so considering that He first made a garden full of nature's beauties and put man in it to enjoy. But it is man who has always ruined the world instead of ruling it. The Preacher, President Solomon David once said, **"God made men and women true and upright: we're the ones who've made a mess of things"** (Ecclesiastes 7:29 TM).

The climate change that is fast becoming a nightmare to the entire world attests to what the erudite scholar, Solomon David rightly observed. The tensions in politics and tussles in leadership are all man-made, resulting in so much disaffections among the global communities. The key players keep dodging the responsibility of addressing them to bring the needed peace and prosperity to their people. Yet, they keep brainstorming options in deceit knowing that they are efforts in futility.

But now, with this renewed call to all and sundry, there must be a change in attitude and coordination in approach to make our world a better place. The attitude of ignoring godly summons to address critical issues that affect us must be dropped. The carefreeness with which we attend to matters of national benefit should give way to a reinvigorated push for their actualization in this dispensation. The nation and indeed the continent have suffered so much humiliation as a result of deliberate delay of the actualization of our hopes and dreams as a people.

The round tables must be set once again, but this time for men and women who have got the badge of honour to discuss our matters and who have the balls to decide in favour of our blessings. We must not continue with people who held us out to global ridicule at the backdrop of our esteemed divine placement on the global stage. We must strive to ensure that those aspiring to take the lead in the emerging generation rewrite our ugly history on pages where every sentence must make sense.

We are blessed and must reclaim our divine heritage. All the woes that have befallen us should not weaken us but wake us up to face the stark realities of our present and prepare us for the future.

Indeed the future is bright but could be bleak if we do not take advantage of my submissions in this book to make our lives better. The betterment of our people to the last man in the remotest clans must become what drives us. Every class of the society must make this their new manifesto.

The Holy bible tells me that the creation awaits the manifestations of the sons of God. I can tell you for sure that those sons of God are here in our country and the African continent with some scattered all over the world. The time of manifestation is at hand; we must not continue to sleep. Sleeping while other global communities are awake is disastrous to our present and can be to the future we dream about.

We have slept enough folks, now it is time to awake and arise so we can take our rightful place among the comity of nations. The voices of the wise and learned must be heard. A paradigm shift is what we urgently need in our leadership. The followers must be incorporated into the governance structures across board even down to the grassroots. No more exclusivity in our systems! The damage it has caused is not worth the deal.

This clarion call is to all and sundry, not just to the representatives of the people. I know that once the people's representatives in government get it right, the result will impact the rest of the people. This is the concept of Trickle Down theory.

However, just as I have done a part of my part in writing this book, we all can do a part in ensuring we heed the call to change the ugly narratives of the African and Nigerian episodes over the years. And this begins at individual levels.

We must not wait for an election year, no, not even until there is a disaster like the Ebola outbreak of some years past or the current Corona Virus pandemic. There is no better time to begin than now. I read of a Chinese proverb that says, *"The best time to plant a tree was twenty years ago. The next best time is now"*.

Let all Nigerians listen to the voice of reason and respond with heart, might and mouth. Africans must imbibe the spirit of fatherland and continue to speak out for truth and justice so we can get to the Promised Land, and that, in time. The people at the grassroots who form the base of the pyramid of society must be ready to form credible and strong alliances to push for the good of the land.

At a time like this, no one should play Adam in a garden already invaded by enemies of our progress. Remember: **"The future will have no pity for those men who possessing the exceptional privilege of being able to speak words of truth to their oppressors have taken refuge in an attitude of passivity, of mute indifference and sometimes of cold complicity"** (Franz Fanon).

Nigeria will succeed. Africa will stand! All glory goes to God – amen.

REFERENCES

All scripture quotations are from the Holy Bible: Authorized King James Version (KJV) unless otherwise stated.

TLB stands for The Living Bible.

TM stands for The Message translation.

NASB stands for New American Standard Bible.

NLT stands for New Living Translation.

AMP stands for Amplified version.

www.ingramcontent.com/pod-product-compliance
Lightning Source LLC
Chambersburg PA
CBHW050010230526
45465CB00003BB/1346